THE WIND

BEFORE YOU START TO READ THIS BOOK, take this moment to think about making a donation to punctum books, an independent non-profit press,

@ https://punctumbooks.com/support/

If you're reading the e-book, you can click on the image below to go directly to our donations site. Any amount, no matter the size, is appreciated and will help us to keep our ship of fools afloat. Contributions from dedicated readers will also help us to keep our commons open and to cultivate new work that can't find a welcoming port elsewhere. Our adventure is not possible without your support.

Vive la Open Access.

Fig. 1. Hieronymus Bosch, *Ship of Fools* (1490–1500)

THE WIND ~ AN UNRULY LIVING. Copyright © 2018 by Jeremy Bendik-Keymer. This work carries a Creative Commons BY-NC-SA 4.0 International license, which means that you are free to copy and redistribute the material in any medium or format, and you may also remix, transform and build upon the material, as long as you clearly attribute the work to the authors (but not in a way that suggests the authors or punctum books endorses you and your work), you do not use this work for commercial gain in any form whatsoever, and that for any remixing and transformation, you distribute your rebuild under the same license. http://creativecommons.org/licenses/by-nc-sa/4.0/

First published in 2018 by punctum books, Earth, Milky Way.
https://punctumbooks.com

ISBN-13: 978-1-947447-95-0 (print)
ISBN-13: 978-1-947447-96-7 (ePDF)

LCCN: 2018963429
Library of Congress Cataloging Data is available from the Library of Congress

Book design: Vincent W.J. van Gerven Oei
Cover photograph: Jeremy Bendik-Keymer

HIC SVNT MONSTRA

Wilkinsburg, Pennsylvania, January 2017

The ~ Wind

*An
Unruly
Living*

Jeremy Bendik-Keymer

*A letter on the political that emerged
from the void, rising with an imaginary
wind, clearing the edges of a society of
possession*

Chagrin Falls, Ohio, May 2017

For Antlers—

> *It comes in the breath of kissing. You must soak up the warmth from those lips, because they are relating only in that emptiness that they eat from out of your lips.*

Airing things * 17

The void * 71

Figures of imagination * 123

To the reader,

In the following pages, you will find at least five forms of writing circling together, usually congruent, sometimes pushing against each other: conceptualization, general scholarship, fiction, lyric, and journaling. Several of these I think of as philosophy—the self-determining and communal search for wisdom through plain thoughtfulness. Others I consider communication that comes *after* or *apart from* philosophy, for philosophy to me is at the end only a contingent and historical practice, tending toward theory, that emerged three thousand years ago across several related cultures around the Aegean Sea. I am trained in philosophy, and profess it at a university, because I think it has been and can be helpful for producing what comes after and apart from it—a community of people who can speak with each other and be thoughtful and accountable in moral relationships. It is particularly the invention of autonomy, authenticity and moral equality that contribute to this, and I see the philosophical tradition as having greatly helped in creating these, but only with the help of religion, literature, art, democracy—and the plain daily intelligence of people.

In this book, wisdom has three names, *vulnerability, delimiting,* and *circumvention,* the topic each of the three studies. What these names invoke will be expressed, explored, and somewhat explained in due course. More than anything, they will be shown and tested.

The three studies are also about *relationship, theory,* and *practice*—the three modes of reason the philosophical tradition has articulated, the first ("relational reason") being the latest to be discovered and still largely inarticulate, despite the constructions and findings of intersubjectivity, phenomenology, hermeneutics, dialogics, psychoanalysis, communicative action, feminist theory, environmental philosophy, and Africana, Chinese, Buddhist, and much Indigenous philosophy. I have written in a more scholarly vein about relational reason elsewhere, as well as having explored it personally in *Solar Calendar, and Other Ways of Marking Time.* You might think of this book as an after-pulse to *Solar Calendar,* a gust after the storm has settled.

As the writing was in *Solar Calendar,* this short stretch of a book is a spiritual exercise (*askēsis*), the ancient philosophical word for a practice of changing yourself or your outlook when doing so involves a reconstruction of your normal life. An exercise of vulnerability is a way of becoming open so that we can be dynamic again. The wind is a figure of dynamism about to come, stirring, unfurling, dispersed, active and alive. Everything becomes alive when we can relate. This is the secret of the void, the solar wind.

~ Jeremy Bendik-Keymer, Buenos Aires, Argentina, September 1st, 2018

Airing things

What should we make of self-ownership? I want to answer this question. Maybe you can help me. To answer it, I need to be vulnerable. And I need a "we," a community. I need someone who can see what I am missing and hear things I'm not hearing. Maybe that can be you.

Self-ownership is the idea that we are owned by ourselves, at least at first. No one else can own us, unless we let them have us. Self-ownership is the idea that we are our own property. We can be traded—but only, initially, by ourselves. If we trade ourselves and give someone else the right to own us, then we can be traded by them, like a piece of property.

Why would we ever want to be treated like a piece of property? All I can come up with is this. There have been people who enslaved other people—the United States of America was founded on slavery. Slavery was only outlawed globally half a century ago. Today, people are still enslaved illegally. Slavery is a large part of human history. Slavery is so oppressive, it is hard to imagine it. People treat other people as something they own.

Imagine that slavery has made your world. Maybe, then, you feel that property is so conflicted, it is hard to be comfortable with it. So you have to do something to make property feel safer. You say that you own yourself. Self-ownership, then, is a response to a world in which property floats in anxiety or foreboding, because of how it is used to abuse people.

The problem is, though, that insisting on self-ownership doesn't change the fact that you are still treating yourself as property. Maybe we should get rid of property. But what would be put in its place?

Good relationships with people. What if self-ownership were only thought up by people, because they are used to bad relationships?

This short book you have in your hands is a book about good relationships. I am interested in seeing some of the ways that self-ownership has gotten into what people think is normal, even right, in my society, which is the United States of America. Self-ownership is like smoke from a fireplace that did not make it out of the chimney. It ends up all over the house. You open a door and find the smell of it. A week later, you put on a shirt, and you smell smoke. The hair of your partner smells of smoke. Only self-ownership doesn't go away with time as smoke does. It is the house itself, the way the house is made and the way neighbors and the police interact with it. Self-ownership is in everything when a society is built on abuse and slavery, that is, on bad relationships.

I want to rebuild my house, not just air it out. But I will start by airing it out and then finding things to take apart— and other things to rebuild. This will take time, I need a community, need others, to complete it. For I am really talking about our common living home, not just mine.

*

I want to take inspiration from the Stoics and explore how to live from a main rule, a *kanōn,* and I want to do so for the sake of finding many of the ways self-ownership has worked into the way I live and where I live. I want my version of the *kanōn* to help me free my way of life from self-ownership. The question is, how can I do this, when the Stoics had such a different way of understanding the world, one that I now do not fully believe is true?

At the heart of Stoic philosophy is the word many ancient philosophers had for "nature," *phūsis*. It is the root of the English word "physical." However, it meant something much more wonderful than the word "physical" sometimes does. Perhaps the way to think about it is like this. When we go outside and run around, playing in the outside, feeling exhilarated by our bodies being full of energy, when we look up at the sky and see a massive cloudbank rolling over the entire land—or water—when we feel the power in us and around us in being physical and in living in this physical world, then that is close to what *phūsis* meant as it was experienced by ancient Greek speakers. *Phūsis* was the power of the cosmos.

The Stoics had a name for their main rule of living. They called the main rule the *kanōn*. It was the rule of living by *phūsis*. When someone was learning to become a Stoic, they did exercises (*askēsis*) in following the *kanōn*. The *kanōn* guided them.

I find that interesting—it makes me want to create something similar that makes sense to me and helps me live without self-ownership. The perplexing thing, though, is to interpret and try to translate the idea of a rule of living by *phūsis*. What is the power of the cosmos?

This is, in many ways, the question many ancient philosophers asked, and they tried to find ways to live with this question, to let their questions and their answers shape their lives. One of the things that they found is that the power of the cosmos is not about owning ourselves—or, for some of them, other people.

The name of the school of philosophers who did the most in this area is "the Stoics," from the ancient Greek word *stōa,* meaning porch. They got their name from philosophizing on a long porch in ancient Athens. They hung out there and talked. The Stoics thought that when we live by *phūsis,* we learn to be part of something cosmic, part of which involves seeing everyone as your equal, equally intelligent and not to be owned. I find the Stoics inspiring for this reason, even if many other things they thought make little sense to me.

*

In order to begin to air things and to experiment with guidance from the Stoics, I want to find where self-ownership has settled by following the experiences I've had in what is often called "nature." In a society of possessions, where to be is to be insecure, sometimes it is helpful to go away from people, literally or inside oneself, to become more open. One of the ways people have done this is by relating to "nature." Here, the word means something different than when we discuss our "nature," and it seems to me something different than *phūsis*. I do not know what to make of that, but it is something I have to consider, something that may form an experiment.

"Nature" is equivocal. But that does not change the fact that, putting words aside, there is something to be said for relating to the elements. I don't think the word "nature" is helpful for many reasons, but I will use it to begin, since it is so resonant to many people. We're discussing the "nature" in which we might submerge ourselves to lose our self-possessed selves and to become renewed.

So that we don't forget that "nature" isn't a very helpful word, though, I will put brackets—" [ ] "—around "[nature]." Perhaps later these brackets will fall away—or the word "nature" will become irrelevant.

*

Now I wonder if living with [nature] can show me what it is like to live without self-ownership? For that to be so, I would need to find a way to live with [nature] that draws on those of its qualities seeming to reveal how self-ownership is conflicted or just plain wrong. It isn't that anything about [nature] immediately frees me from the problems of self-ownership. I have to relate to [nature] in helpful ways to free myself up. I have to do something creative with the way that I live to find the benefits of living with [nature]. What I have to do is like an experiment or a test. I have to try something to see what results I get or make something up that works for me as I go. The Stoics called this an *askēsis,* a philosophical exercise.

*

I will take, then, one part of [nature], or what the Stoics would think of as one expression of *phūsis,* to be my guide. The wind. I want to see what kind of life I could live if I took the wind as a rule of living.

The wind airs things. It is fluid. It appears on Earth when the movement of air—never stopping—quickens to a point where we notice it. The wind is always related to us. While air moves regardless of us, when we feel it, air becomes wind. The wind is a relative. It is already close to us.

The wind is close to us, but in such a way that it takes us outside ourselves. Even if we shut ourselves up in a building with a swift wind circling around outside, our attention is always drawn to the outside by the wind. If we are outside and feel the wind, we find ourselves on the edge of our skin. In this way, the wind will not let us own ourselves. It exposes us. The wind is a relative that reveals to us that we are vulnerable. Because of this, I think the wind is a good way to show what living by *phūsis* could be. There's much to make of it.

I want to see what happens: I want to learn from the wind as a relative. I want to walk around in the wind. I want to hear it over my roof at night. I want to remember what it is to have no roof. I want to be afraid of the trees falling down, see the blowing leaves across the road, later the churning snow in the air. I want my heart to go out to those who must face a hurricane and have the courage to save their lives. I want to remember what the wind can do and be grateful for human kindness in the face of what it has done. I want the sound and sight of the wind over the land where I live make me wonder with my eyes open and my skin a vibrant mind. I want my body to become alive from the touch of this relative. I want to curse it when it makes it hard for me to run. I want to be glad when it makes it easier for me to run, pushing, pushing. I want my invention of wind to feel like an explosion of movement out of a quiet home into the open yard, the street, the park.

I want to forget myself in the wind, to find the trees outside tossing larger than anything on my mind. I want to be connected to you and to every animal. I want us all to be encircled by the wind. I want to be connected to the rest of the planet. I want to share something with everyone. I want to be equal to anyone and to everything, even a gorge of rock tossed and eroded by the wind. The current of the stream in the gorge of rock, the clouds in the sky moving across it in a sudden standing pool, rippled by motion, fluid on fluid, liquid on air.

It isn't that the wind makes me do anything, although I may have to resist it in order to do what I want or even in order to be. It's that the wind is a relative that I can relate with in order to disown the idea that the world is carved up by pieces of property. The wind can help me make something good of [nature], even though [nature] is itself neither good nor bad; it simply is. By the wind simply moving, I can make something of the fact that it can't care about us at all. Yet it can relate us to each other.

*

There is one thing interesting to me when I think about my rule. It is that the wind cannot be a rule. I think the wind does not rule; it is unruly. Property is ruly, wind unruly. Calculating how to do things is ruly; relationships are unruly. Our beliefs can be orderly, but relationships are disorderly—surprising us at every real turn of their story. To meet someone cannot be made or thought in advance. To meet someone requires openness. To be personal is to be vulnerable. It is not to be turned into an object of any kind by rules of thought or rules of behavior. Being good to each other involves keeping our word, but keeping our word isn't something that is predictable and regularly measured. A promise has a story of how we keep it, a personal story, with twists and turns, hopes and regrets, with some sadness sometimes and often an exuberant generosity, like jumping off a spinning play-wheel, falling to the ground, dizzy, laughing, mildly sick. No, the wind is an unruly living.

Not long ago, I was sitting in school, wondering why we were only reading books. The books were about living, but all we did is talk about them. The books were written in words so big and abstract, there was no human warmth to them. They were as cold as a hospital morgue's floor, but with less emotion in the cracks. I wondered why we only read books and usually only books that are impersonal. What can you learn about living from words that have no trace of the life they led about them? Words live lives, coming out of the mouths of people who live lives. Words are made by people, and they make us people when we speak them to each other.

I wanted to trust the books by knowing the life of their words and the people who made them. So I decided that I would not sit still when the books are supposed to hold everything in their place and make us become impersonal. I decided to become unruly.

In this, I was learning from wind. One of the things I like about wind is that it is a void that we cannot avoid. Wherever it is, it is pushing us off our balance or drawing us out of ourselves. When we feel it, it has already moved us. Where we now are is where we were not. Our presence is led by an absence. Wind is a void we cannot avoid.

Wind is thus what it feels like to meet someone. To meet someone is to be moved. Where you both are now is where you were not then. The presence of this person makes your past life absent. You rush into the void and meet.

A person that you meet is a void whom you cannot avoid. Meeting opens life to movement, a house unlocked to air with a bright, Fall day outside. Even if everything stays in place, everything is different. Choose to air things!

*

The writing in your hands, before your eyes, in your ears (?) is the thing I can show you to show that there is a way to turn wind into philosophy. But what if wind's philosophical trick is to avoid being shown at all? Then I would write a book about the wind, missing it entirely, write about nothing almost, talking around and around in circles like an eddying, empty bag of potato chips scuttling across the street and toward someone's lawn.

What can I do? But I am not going to do it. I'm not going to write about the wind. I am going to write *from* it. My unruly rule is this thing I call, "vulnerability." It will be my way to show the wind, like a sheet hung out to air that fills, billows, until a corner slips off and the sky hangs swaying in light.

There is really no way to do this than to air things. Airing things it the way writing becomes vulnerable. But what is vulnerability?

*

In an age of property, I love vulnerability. In an age of mine and thine, I love relationship. In a world where everything is someone's object to use or to observe, I love ways to relate personally.

When you approach things practically, you try to figure out what to do with them and how to get done what you want to get done. You talk about objectives and obstacles. You have an object of action. You use things to get things done. When you look at the world theoretically, you want to figure out what to believe is true about the world. You look at objects and observe them. You think about your ideas of them. You figure out what you can know about them.

But if you look at people like this, you will never get to know them, even if you know a lot about them. To know someone, you have to relate. Similarly, if you try to get to know a person by manipulating them, by treating them as an objective or as an obstacle, you will never know them as a person, because you will not even be treating them as a person.

To relate to things, however, is to get to know them as you would a person. It isn't to do anything with them or even to know a lot about them. It's to be with them, personally. So they enter your dreams, just as people do. I see the wind like this; my unruly rule of living with the wind is a relating.

*

This book you have in your hands is unruly and strange. I apologize if it causes you confusion. But would you allow me to say that confusion can sometimes be good? Maybe part of the society of self-possession is that we should not appear confused and so we avoid it. But isn't the society of possession confusing? Doesn't it work against our nature?

Maybe we don't know what nature is. I agree with Giovanni Pico della Mirandola that our "nature" is to transform our "nature." We are creatures who remake ourselves. Self-possession may be one version of that. But why does it seem so inhuman?

It does seem possible that people in my society could be more openly who they are. It does seem that a society of self-possession cuts against the nature of relationships, undercutting who *we* are. But who are we? Who are we in relationships?

*

About two hundred years ago, a little more and a little less, there were some writers in France who thought it made perfect sense to live "naturally." The Swiss philosopher Jean-Jacques Rousseau was their inspiration for the most part, and the writer Stendhal was the best example of them. Stendhal used to write of *le naturel.* It was an attitude, a way of living.

The idea behind the "natural" was that people should not be so caught in their manners that they do not express and trust their feelings that express care for themselves. Most people grow up being taught ways to behave, what is right and wrong, good and bad to do. Even if our parents don't use these words, their own behavior teaches us what they are about. When our parents disapprove of something strongly, we learn that it is wrong; when they are glad and content with another thing, we learn that it is right. When they are eager for something, we learn that it is good, and when they avoid or wish something wouldn't happen, we learn that it is bad.

Rousseau and Stendhal thought that we shouldn't get so bothered by what is right or wrong, good or bad according to our parents, priests, and professors that we don't listen to how we feel we can care for ourselves and trust it. Suppose I feel agitated sitting in my seat listening to a person speak at me for an hour. My brain is shutting down, and I am not absorbing anything. Suppose I also think that it is wrong of me to get up and leave, that it would be impolite. If I were "natural," I would listen to my feelings and act on them. I'd get up and step out, take some air, then see how I feel. I wouldn't relate to where I am as if it is a prison. I wouldn't relate to my feelings as if I need to be kept in prison. I wouldn't try to possess myself.

I like this idea. Obviously, I like it. But I don't think calling what it's about "natural" makes sense. Even if I listen to my feelings, I still have to decide to listen to them. Relating to myself is an act; it is decisive. That means I have to value it, think that it is good or even right. Listening to myself seems a deeper form of politeness.

There's also the problem that the French writers of the "natural" often contrasted the "natural" with the "social" or the "conventional." It was as if learning how to get along with others and share some ways to be together were somehow "unnatural." What did "unnatural" then mean? If it means that sharing life together needs to be one where people can't trust their feelings, that is false. When people have good relationships, they learn to trust their feelings more, not less.

If, then, being "unnatural" meant not being found in "nature," that is also false. We humans live together. Being "social" is part of our "nature." Perhaps, then, these writers meant that we somehow do not live according to [nature] when we don't listen to our feelings? If that is so, it's not clear what [nature] means. For one, it isn't the same [nature] as was found with the Stoics, because they didn't want people to listen to their feelings. Still, they thought that there is a cosmic [nature] that can guide us.

The point is, the notions of the "natural" and of [nature] are confusing. This is why I have not let them stand in writing but have put different kinds of marks around them. Things are swirling!

*

I think that it is time to be clearer. Being clear feels good. From the Stoics and their *phūsis,* I will take the idea that there is a cosmos that is awesome. When I glimpse it for a moment—and it is always hard for me to do more than glimpse it—it rises as a wave, more powerful and vast, more intricate—then complex—more puzzling and striking, far more than I could have imagined. It is around me and beyond me. It is in me and moves me. I disappear in it and cannot even do the thing I am doing right now, which is thinking! This [nature] is wonder at the whole of the universe moving in its own way and with everyone and everything I know in it with me in it too, still the universe, beyond all of us and all of what I can think.

From the French writers of two hundred years ago, I take the idea of a deeper politeness. This deeper politeness includes trusting ourselves and being open about what we feel. Such self-trust is not easy in a society of self-ownership. To have to own yourself is to fear that someone else might own you. Self-ownership is afraid. This fear sinks into oneself. There on the outside of self-ownership, like a double-image that you rub your eyes to erase, is the fear. I don't have an easy time understanding how to trust myself in such a place. The fear is so close in everything, molding it. Worry is a part of me.

The deeper politeness would say that I owe it to myself to separate out of the fear that comes from my society from the feelings of how I can care for myself and how I can be. I deserve to be more care-free. If I am then open about what I feel, I have become courageous. In my society, people are afraid of each other deep down. Open, I become vulnerable.

*

Phūsis challenges self-ownership too. There is no obvious reason, other than a word—"nature"—to link *le natural* with *phūsis*. The cosmos and deep politeness are very different things. Even as a word about the cosmos, *phūsis* is still wonder opened onto the great universe that exceeds us in every wave of elemental force. By contrast, *le naturel* is a word about how we might trust ourselves and be open with each other. It is part of our life, not the great life around us that came before us and will continue long, long after us.

But from the standpoint of my goal to live by the wind as an elemental force that suggests a way beyond self-ownership, there is much to say about joining the cosmos and deep politeness. Let me say some of it.

First of all, the intuition behind deep politeness is that the things we feel, arising within us and along our bodies, are as real as the elements outside in the air and are guides to how to live caringly this life. If *phūsis* is a name for the elemental, *le naturel* is a name for what is elementary about our feelings.

The emotions are waves. They come from things and get at things—before we know them. Born out of the ways we have been weathered as beings and then again as lives, they display the outside to which we may respond if we are aware and responsible enough to not simply react.

If to live by *phūsis* is to thoughtfully frame one's decisions with the elemental universe that is so vast and powerful as to outstrip one's control in every sense, to live from *le naturel* is to make room in one's life for uninhibited expressions of how one is finding the things of this world. The life of the world comes to us through our feelings. Our feelings show us our relations. Through them we are already outside ourselves, in the midst of life. *Phūsis* frames us, whereas *le naturel* unframes us. They are two motions that undo self-absorption.

Deep politeness is elemental in being open, and the elements are deeply polite because of their capacity to frame us within a larger whole!

The cosmos opens up a space inside us, while emotions show us how the cosmos moves.

We cannot own the cosmos, nor can it own us, it is indifferent. When it opens up inside us, it displaces the patterns of ownership. Similarly, when the cosmos moves through our emotions, they are not things we have, but ways that we are. Moreover, they are us relating, not possessing. They share in the wider circulation of things.

The cosmos circulates us. Our emotions follow, born of the weather patterns in our minds, our own cosmic space.

The way I see it, *phūsis* and *le naturel* are two different ideas about how we might circumvent our self-possession. This word, "circumvention," will be another important word of this book. Circumvention, as I understand it, is the wind's word for practical wisdom. With circumvention comes practical wisdom, and by learning how to circumvent ourselves, we are more or less wise.

I imagine myself a clown in a designer suit. My hair is green and sticking out at angles. My beard is long and blue, with red streaks running down its length below my chin.

I have to be put together for my business meeting. I have to get a family to sign a contract. My bank will be lending them money. I have to be convincing, even though I know that my bank has played a trick on them. They will almost surely get into a tight, financial spot with my bank.

I must keep it together so that they sign their lives into the order of possession and let us set the clock to their dispossession.

But my hair is giving me away. My beard is, too. I can't contain them—they are my given colors.

The family is getting nervous; they sense that something is off.

I cannot take it anymore—I tear up the contract and cry into their arms. They think I am insane, but they have been saved for a time.

Meanwhile, I am lost, but outside as I ride to the hospital strapped to a gurney, there are stars far up in the galaxy. I see them through the ambulance window. They look coldly on me and wink. Even in my wild-haired state, I am not alone in the universe. Rather, everything is rising to the void.

Both *phūsis* and *le naturel* approach circumvention through vulnerability, first and foremost by working out two ends of a relationship that we need in order to be free of any locked-up self-possession. *Le naturel* unworks self-possession inside ourselves, making our pressure to turn ourselves into normal objects dissipate in acts of spontaneous and surprising dispossession. *Phūsis* addresses self-absorption outside ourselves, revealing the density with which we turn inward and away from the cosmos as a form of avoidance, a wished-for invulnerability. Then, we cannot be infinitely in control of ourselves inside. Nor can we be the totality of everything in the world.

*

When philosophy appeared, the ancient Greek world of Athens was dissected by exclusions, among the most important of which were created by possession. Slaves, women, territories.

The Roman empire did not fundamentally alter these exclusions except in form, regulation, and reach. Slaves, women, lands still were owned, and their owning defined the world as it was ruled. In such a place and time, the cosmos was a fantasy of something beyond control. It was dispossession, the great equalizing, the total sharing. There was nothing you could do about it. You were subject to *phūsis*. Even the emperor was. He could not outrun its fate or break its power. That was how Stoicism understood things.

The literary world of the late 18th and early 19th centuries in Europe and America—a time and culture historians often call "Romantic"—was no stranger to possession. Slavery formed the trans-Atlantic reach of it.

Outside Europe, the colonies sucked out life and labor, heedless of their twisted abuse.

In America, the possessive society of Europe recreated itself. Even free of European power, European Americans still colonized, and European Americans still slaved.

Is it a sick joke to think of Romantic people learning to live by *le naturel* next to the degraded life of slaves and the effacement and murder of the colonized? Here they are, the great spontaneous ones, enjoying their feelings and the cosmos inside!

But *le naturel* plays a trick on this sick joke, it has the last laugh. Inside it is a memory of a life where we should not wall off ourselves to our feelings and the movements of our bodies. And there now all around *are* bodies with feelings.

When you let yourself be vulnerable, these fellow body souls split open the cosmos itself with family-shattering trauma, daily suffering, determination in travail, resilience, craft, just and overwhelming rage. Oh, to be "natural" is to be naturally disarmed—to be open to facing the costs of possession all around: a history of writhing bodies and discarded time.

*

It is important to understand that there is not anything about the wind that must make us think these things. The wind does not have to be cosmic to you, and it does not have to suggest a deeper politeness. There are things one can make of the wind, figures of imagination. The Stoics made something of the cosmos. They fashioned a rule of living. Some French romantics made something of the feeling of being outdoors, far from society. They imagined a way of letting go and experimented with it. I am at work on a problem that bothers me deep in my society and in my society's history.

I want to make of the wind an unruliness around self-ownership. This is not *description* of the wind. It could be poetry made into politics, and why not? Why shouldn't we figure the way to becoming more fully related and alive by being vulnerable? The way of relationships is a far cry from slavery. I figure this way through the wind.

So that to which I am in relationship is not "[nature]." It is a possibility, really. I figure on in listening to and feeling the wind as a cosmic element. It suggests to me a deeper politeness with myself, I cannot ignore the conflicted guidance of my feelings and the way they make me vulnerable. The wind is in this way a revelatory figure.

This too. The wind is a figure of a vulner-

Later, I was alone in my hospital room. No friends came to see me. My green hair, my blue and red beard were tufting the white gown and sheets, a halo of light on the pale green tiles of the walls from the dim night illuminations on the opposite wall by the sink. The voids sat around me, and I could hear the air outside circumventing the building. It was winter, icy, dry and whistling quietly.

I said, "My friends, I can no longer be who I have tried to be. I am a travesty of a person. The suit I've worn is made of the sobbing of parents, late at night behind their bedroom doors where their kids won't hear. I cannot contain that order of possession anymore. I am sorry."

One of my void-friends, the kindest one, said, "You do not have to do those things. This is better. It is so infinitely better to abandon that pain and calculation and throw it to the void."

When she said this, I started crying again, more grateful than I had been in a long, long time since, it felt, I was a child and ran around in the summer grass.

No one else said a thing. Outside, the wind rose to a moan for a moment and then subsided. It was crystalline outside, and the lights in the parking lot were almost blue in the dark.

ability that appears before, with, and after relationships in which my soul is free.

*

What does the wind reveal? The void. The void is where my soul is free and where each of my relationships is clear and meaningful when I think of it.

The void will not be anyone's possession, and the idea of possessing another person in the void is a delusion.

The void makes any attempt to possess another a futile obsession. The void dissipates the political orders founded on self-possession and the possession of lands and rule of peoples—it scatters them to grief.

In the void, all people are free, and all beings alive on Earth come into being and strive to find their weathering.

The void is real only as delimitation. It is the mother of wise belonging, and makes all relationships rare in their own way, reaching us, if we let them, in a way that we hadn't felt, ache to ache, an impulse of emptiness.

Don't avoid, then, the void. My figure of imagination will be vulnerable in it. I'll be dispossessed.

I am unruly and cannot find a way to rule others.

Even to let others be ruled voids my heart.

We cannot even rule ourselves—we relate.

Society as I know it is unworked, flying apart bit by bit until it floats in shambles of things where once there were relationships or still could be. Even democracy will break and bend. Only the people, like an open-ended cyclone—gathering, rising, circling, falling, swirling, then flying apart—collect here. They demand a world free of possession, because anything else is delusional.

In a fire, the sparks swirl in swift channels toward the sky, piercing the background dark with puncture of ancient stars. The void is that dark; the stars are dispossessions. Only in their extinction is there a space where we can listen.

When I left the hospital, my mother met me. She was old and struggling with age. She looked upset.

"Why have you done this?"

She almost shouted at me.

I could feel the old fear in my body. It was the fear of not living up and the fear of going back all at once. It was the cold feeling that I would not be able to explain myself.

"Mom, can we go get some food? There's a restaurant nearby. It should be quiet there."

"All right." Curt, like she could not be bothered.

But she was listening. I sensed it with my body. It was as if there were a split-second delay between her words and her look, as if in between that self-possession, born of her apparent anger at my foolishness, she was genuinely concerned. Was I all right? Would I be?

I thought to myself, "Every relationship is singular. There are no two exactly alike. She is listen-

The wind scatters them away. And we are here. What will we find meaningful?

I want to learn from the wind as I would learn from the void. But what is it to learn from wind? My thought is that it is to let myself be vulnerable. The wind, then, would be found in the ways my vulnerability became clear, broken out from self-possession by the work of dispossession. Wind's traces would be there in the moving relationship.

There, they would arise through unruliness shaking free the next turn of the relationship.

I have to look, even more, start feeling. The body's intelligence will be multitude when encircled with void, with wind.

*

At the heart of self-possession is distrust of oneself, starting with one's body and its feelings. Certainly, the body is limited and often misleading. Yes, our feelings can be mistaken or focused on bad things which we think we want or want to do. There is nothing perfect about the body or its senses, the soul and its emotions. But all the same, what we feel, especially in our bodies, can tell us much. If it is misdirection, it is rich misleading. What it says is full of reality, if only the realness of our delusions.

The point about feelings, and our body, isn't about their ability to tell us true—or false—things. It's about the way that they are helpful if there are to be relationships. If we can't feel, we can't relate emotionally. If we don't let

ing, and I am reaching out to her. She senses it. She wants me to reach her, hopes somewhere that in that touchless touch, she can let go of her anxiousness."

I thought, "I am a different person now, nearer the one I used to be as a child, running through the summer grass!

"But I am also strangely aged. I have circumvented myself. I must circumvent her worry—speak with her beyond self-possession. After all, she gave birth to me from the void."

ourselves relate emotionally, we don't relate as richly, fluidly, and cosmically as humans can. Our relations may not even be personal at all.

If we are disembodied, we can hardly feel. Thus, we are constrained in our relation. It will not be personal at all.

*

Once when I was little, I remember walking into my mother's room as she was making up her face in the mirror. The room was aqua-grey, submerged in the industry of her care of herself. The wallpaper had small wild flowers on it, all in shades of that underwater color. Her mirror was illuminated by cool, white lights at either side, and her face glistened in them. She was focused on her eyeliner, and she looked down at me from her work through the mirror, an arch of the eyebrow above the eye she was designing.

"Will you be a good boy and be a gentleman someday? I can see you pleasing your mama." It made me nervous. I didn't know what she meant. I felt that my mother wanted me to be rich and shiny, like the man who would come to pick her up at the front door not much later once my sitter had arrived.

But my green hair looked ridiculous. I knew that. Everyone teased me about it at school. And yet I wouldn't dye it, not on my life. It was as if a part of me would not give up the way I had come into the world.

I think that it was at that moment, or during that time of my young life, that I decided to be rich and powerful. I saw the men in the magazines dressed in silken suits. I felt their self-possession and their projection of power over everyone and everything, their ability to know how to navigate the maze of society and to always come out the exit leaving poor, confused losers behind. I saw that while they were not omnipotent, they were able to use the order of possessions to protect themselves. I felt that they would save me and please my mother.

I felt these things for years and forgot them. They became a part of me.

When I collapsed, they came back to me in the hospital, and I realized that although they were ill and delusional, they were real and took me back to the mirror of myself where I saw the void that had made me shrink back and try to possess my fate.

Sitting by the blanched outdoors, her face side-lit by a thick, large, plate-glass window, my mother's skin was almost see-through. The blue veins ran along it.

It was wrinkled more minutely than a cellophane, blue wrapper.

She was tense under that membrane, balled and ready for flight. Her eyes were recessed and would not settle on mine. She was in pain seeing me, but she was not feeling it.

For a moment, I went back to how I felt as a boy when she would look at me from her mirror and judge. I remember freezing each time, caught in her proscription, the words silently sent through her eyes.

I remember crawling back inside myself until my body was a shell, and I was a green-haired, plastic doll. From its plastic face, something looked back at her, but not I, for I was gone.

Something would have thrown myself out of the window if she had said so.

Something would have projected me out into the summer air, falling alongside the shards and splinters of glass, the bits of wooden frame, the amber fireflies dodging and the cicadas suddenly quiet in the trees.

Something was staring back at her. It said, "yes."

Where was I? It didn't matter. Something moved my body again, "Yes," and her eyes shifted back to the mascara.

*

What happens to many of us instead is that we trust our bodies only so much, let them tell us how we feel somewhat and to a point. Similarly, we feel things and let them show us where we are—to a degree. Thus we relate somewhat, to a point, only so much, to a degree. This may be prudent, but it depends on how well we have learned to care for ourselves through our senses.

Still, it is this way with relation: we have to let ourselves in for relations to begin. They will be imperfect—this much is perfectly clear—and they will involve fantasies, delusions, wishes, distortions, mean-spirited stuff—anger, envy, callousness, deflection—avoidance, shame, fear, and ... but have I said enough? They will feel bad in many ways. Still, they will be relations. If we avoid facing ambivalence in ourselves and abandon all these feelings, we have decided not to relate as fully as the universe affords us.

This is what it means to realize that the form of a relationship is unconditional, even if the people in it cannot be, because they are all too human and limited. The relationship assumes an unconditional origin by which all that we feel is relevant, because it is what we feel. Only on its basis can we fully relate. In the falsity of its scraps is a deeper truthfulness.

Thus you can see, I hope, why the name I give for the wind is the void. The void carries everything. It is unconditional.

Similarly, the cosmos is unconditional—out of indifference.

So, too, with deep politeness—its impulsiveness cannot subject the soul to conditions on where it is and how it feels.

*

Years later, I understood, to a point, how she had to battle men for her self-possession, starting by seeing if her look would possess them. She could not let her guard down on a night when an alliance was possibly being worked out.

Later, however, she would return, come to my side as I was sleeping, the sitter having been dismissed. Sometimes I would fake being asleep to see how she was with her guard down. She would often run her hand on my hair and hum. Then, for a moment, she loved my green hair. As she let herself feel, she would sound distracted, somewhere far off, as if she could take off her shoes and walk in the grass or with her cousins when they were young on her maternal grandparent's farm, tucked into the valley not far from the mines.

I wished she would look at me from her mirror with that hum, look through her closed eyes so that we could communicate.

*

I am finding a current. The wind rose and now rushes through the limbs of the orchard in my mind. Some branches have even split, and their winter apples have rolled along the hardened ground into gullies, roots, and dips. The icy trees shine in the sun the next morning, crystal patterns on the eyes of those who pass, human or small mammal.

It is time to let the distortion and the fantasy become a source of realness. To say these things is not to possess truths. Only the truly foolish know where and when relationship. I must slip, crack my head, and be vulnerable to the fact that I am truly, am.

You see, the thing that will blow open the shutters and the doors of self-ownership is relationship. That is why it comes with the wind. Is the wind the void, or is it relationship—or is it the change that happens when self-ownership becomes dispossessed? The wind is equivocal within this space. It has many meanings. They swirl away and reappear with the pull of the void to release people, lands, and other beings from the society of possession's in-grown self-possession. The wind itself cannot be owned, not even in its meaning. But it has lent itself to figure a different way into this life, and now I move along with it through my imagination, seeking the way of relationship that tears through the structures of the landowners, the slavers, and the factories until there is a different way of being in this life beyond calculating, subjecting, and producing.

The wind shorts the systems beneath the servers too, until there is another way to be human than to competitively invest in ways to out-profit your fellow person. The wind is a political-economic fantasy that figures relationship. In this, there is equality.

*

You might wonder how. All you need do is to think of the void. The void is unconditional. In it, that you feel, how you do, and what you feel are not denied. It isn't a matter of doing something with them, of acting or of acting on them, but of their being. Only in that starting point can there be a relationship.

But with whom? With another, or with others, who relate.

Yet they too must be able to relate. They, too, must be in a void, unconditionally. Otherwise, they cannot relate.

And if they cannot relate, you will have no relationship either. It takes more than one to form a relationship.

Unconditional void to unconditional void—ache to ache—there is—there must be—equality, or there will be no relationship, not truly.

Another way to put that is this: if you, accepting yourself in deep politeness and with the indifference of the cosmos seeing that and how you are, are to relate truly, then you must meet others with whom you relate. Relationships go both ways, shifting back and forth as on a current of air. They disrupt and reconfigure and cannot be determined from one source. Well, then you need to be as open to that one with whom you relate as you were to your own soul, possibly more. The risks of being conditional are high when you face the different mind of another person. You must be a void to them. There will be no possession.

*

Now that I have become a villain of this society and a hero of another, I often dream of dismantling the city in my thoughts, straight from science-fiction. In my dream, I literalize a mindfulness exercise I once read. The city is taken apart block by block to reveal only the plumbing. I know that I confuse the image with a two-page story I once read, of a city of only plumbing where the showers turn on and off, water spraying from several stories to the ground, although no hand is there to turn them and no head is there to be washed over by the warmth.

In the exercise, I begin by circumventing time. The first block to be removed is the clock. The time of the new society is the time of the fulfilling meeting. It is like the Indian measure of the breath as musical time-keeping. Take as long as it takes to have a relationship.

Then I un-build the roads, railways, and airports, asking how they could be given time.

I change the market into a long, drawn-out process of finding the "enough"—for the day, the week—but otherwise is modest.

The schools are great curiosities, too. Everything has been changed from production to relationship. I no longer try to beat you. Instead, we play together as we investigate the great unclarity that is a part of the cosmos itself.

This new city is made of people who meet fresh from a mystery. The mystery is the vulnerability they feel now that they do not need to produce themselves and fear their competitors. They are in touch with the outside, and this makes them equal in their openness.

*

I find that when wind goes through my mind, I am spacey. I'm an air head. The words swirl about and are not precise. It is muddled thinking. Yet if I let myself sort out, the words falling about the place, I also begin to find something that, to an extent, defies words, allowing me to work off of them and to rearrange them in creative ways.

There is an old distinction in Latin between a disagreement *de dicto* and a disagreement *de re*. The former is a confusion over words; it is semantic. The Latin means "about what is said." The latter is a difference over facts; it is about reality. The Latin means "about the thing." Wind, I find, often causes *de dicto* turbulence but leads to *de re* clarity.

The clarity I find with the wind is the clarity of the way the cosmos appears from the perspective of relating. In such a perspective, the same openness that is the cosmos around us opens up within us as the unconditional validity of how and what we sense. "Validity," here, does not mean accuracy, because our feelings are so often confused. It means instead that without seeing that what we sense is a part of a relationship, we cannot relate truly or truthfully. Any relationship will have to work through distortions, but without it being open, it will not be, truly, a relationship.

The world appears differently from relationship. It is not something primarily to be manipulated. It is not something to be *done*. Nor is it something to get our heads around and figure out, at least primarily. It is not something that must in the first instance be believed, as if all we had to do at first is doubt where and that we are. In relationship, the world appears primarily as something to be sensed so that it can be touched, or better yet, reached. From this touch, we may then know and we may then do. But the primary thing is the intimacy that develops over time, confidently. It is about trust, not believing.

And there is no trust. My society is a disaster. It is a not-star, a void of light, hope, direction, and wonder. The word *disaster* comes from the word for a star in Latin. The prefix, *dis-*, means that the star has been erased. A disaster is a thing without a star. It is the anti-cosmic, for the cosmos is the void filled with stars. And since stars are our beacons when travelling on the sea or by land with no other navigation, since they are visual metaphors for hope and are causes of wonder, to live in a disaster is to lack these things, at least when we look out and up at night.

In my society, it is stupid to trust. This is what self-possession born of the possession of others brings. "Hear me," we say, "trust is the great foolishness." Where is trust when a twelve year old, Black boy can be shot by society's protectors in less than two seconds of their seeing him standing around doing nothing in a park, a toy gun by his side? They say that he had the orange safety tip removed, but they could not see the toy gun; he was doing nothing threatening, and they did not stop to ask him to confirm that the gun was just a toy. They said nothing, my society's protectors who protect the order of possession. They shot and killed him without a second thought—or even a first. They shot in less time than it takes to find and press a "like" on social media.

"What trust?" If you have the self-possessions—the wealth—you can think that you are safe—until you no longer have that wealth. Of course, if you come from the people who were possessed in slavery, or if you are of the lineages of those whose lands were possessed, your wealth will not fully protect you, not even conditionally. You may still be stopped by the protectors of the order of possession, frisked, assaulted. You may still carry a history of violence inside you that makes it easy for you to feel depressed and worthless. You may still not know how you can exist in society, since the order of possession is fundamentally an order of violent not voluntary dispossession—taking land and life from people and places.

All these things we carry in our bodies. Those most at risk carry these things most. But everyone carries them somewhere. In a society where it is fundamentally acceptable to let people die if they do not have possessions, it is never actually safe. The unconditional source of the void is kept out of mind, because society is so conditional. The relations are entirely practical and—if you are strategic—theoretical. The relational has to be kept down.

*

The loss of the relational is in our bodies. It is in us as distrust. The cost of self-possession is the loss of the relational. The burden of self-possession is distrust.

When we walk down the street, we cannot trust each other.

If we are out driving, we have to be defensive.

In shopping, people push by you, reaching for things to possess.

Out in a diner, you can stare at your

It was clear, for example, that my mother loved me but did not love herself. Because I was free, she no longer had a mirror to protect her in me. My "insanity" made these things obvious.

So I said, "Mom, it doesn't matter anymore that I won't be a banker and will have to transform my life into something more modest. What matters is that you are seeing me here, and I am seeing you. This is where we are now before we walk into the void."

coffee or at your text message screen. Side to side is avoidance.

At school, the question is who will beat you—on the test or on the playground?

Who would be so stupid as to trust?

In this space, the wind can only be thought of as a moment when the society of distrust falls down, roiling apart to let something else suddenly appear.

The thing that is so hard, that cries out like bad weather in the tossing trees, is the loss of unconditional safety next to the memory and bruised hope of a vulnerable and trusting meeting. How can you put the two together? They are together painful, because both are true. It is practically and obviously true that there is a lack of safety in my society. It is relationally true that without vulnerability, there will be nothing worth living for, because I will not be able to relate to anything, thereby voiding its possible worth to me. It is painful to live in this split open reality. But the wind rushes through it.

You see, in airing things, I come to a position that makes hope more basic than distrust, and I have no evidence that it is actually so in my society. Indeed, I think that it isn't so—maybe, that it can't be. I only have the shape of "us" instead. If there is no relating, there is no point to possessing, because the possessions do not actually mean something to you truly. They are, strictly speaking, meaningless without your relation to them. But if there is no point to possession, there is no point to the struggle to possess, which is the source of distrust. So, relating must be for meaningful things to be. And if relating is, there must be hope—for meaning, intimacy, and trust.

*

What, anyway, is the point of possession? It is to ward off people from taking your things—and ultimately from taking yourself. The idea behind possession is self-protection.

What is the point of self-protection? It is to keep yourself free to live well.

But why have a good life? To enjoy it, to find it meaningful, to experience life, to do the right thing, to create.

So the point of possession is the same as that of relating with this one exception: self-possession leads to the threat of violent dispossession. It is contradictory. It trusts in distrust. So it loses trust. And yet we are stuck on it?

The simpler way to be is to relate.

Like this. I have made something of the wind, I have related to it so that it is a relative.

*

But what does the wind think? When it is airing things, how is it feeling? What would it be for it to relate to us?

The wind is indifferent, physical, and without consciousness of any kind. When I relate to it, I personify it, projecting my anthropomorphic fantasies. No, the wind is the void of anything we call human, except the parts of us that are void-like.

The wind sees me as a density. It moves around me and moves me. It is going somewhere else. Would I like to follow? My wool hat already has. I was running with it, but now it is following with the wind, blown

When I was a banker, I could never look people in the eyes unless I was acting. I had to keep guarded about what was really going on in the numbers and figure out how the people were lying or almost lying in their requests for investment and attests of reliability. My green hair helped, because they would be distracted. Something could manipulate them easily then, and I would hide deep inside myself where even the Something that appeared to be me couldn't find me.

Often, my hands would be cold, even in the warm office.

along the street. That damn hat. That damn wind!

But I am talking about myself again. The wind has moved past my hat and is onto the neighbor's trees. They are also densities, but they are flexible. The wind has shaken them side to side as it went beyond them. The wind is always going somewhere else. It is at the next point, not this one. It's never where we are—it is where it wants to go.

Somewhere, blocks from here, the wind subsides. The air is equal and calm. Like a bad mood, or a good one, the wind—

Part of relationship is understanding that they are just gone, sometimes, the relatives.

*

And here I have brought us to a state, a strange state, where it is not clear what we are talking about anymore. We've left the ground. There's nothing solid to know. The words are fluid and shifting, and they rush by on an errant course. The mind feels dispossessed, recoils or rebels, the words are pointless and the book is useless. The claims are baseless, and the idea is nothing but a cloud. The de-pressuring of words has begun. They seek a level whose meaning is vague and shifting, shifting so minutely as to be almost unmoving.

*

The wind is the localizing agent. As it circles around the body, coming into clothes—or as it crashes and slides over buildings leaving a dull whistle—as the house is for a moment not a home, and then it is a home protecting you from the wind—as the leaves and limbs outside tell you the day is floating, keep you alive inside by the movement, there, in the trees, grasses and bush—as things roll along the sidewalk outside hurrying nowhere, hurrying—the mind comes into focus out of void. Its dull poetry is voluntary dispossession.

*

At the most inside point of vulnerability is a suffering that cannot be escaped. The loss of a child by a society's callousness is the single evidence that the society is a moral disaster. Nothing will void the cruel vacuum. So we rush and hurry past it, or let the dull ache of it seep through our bodies and be lost. It's this way avoidance works. Avoidance is a daily distraction and a passable sorrow become our sense of reality.

The void dreams are not figures, they are absences, absences so absent you forget that they are absorbing all light like black holes. You just live in a dimmer reality, the grey day bent toward night. The void dreams come with the possessions, and they help us avoid the disaster we call "home."

The void dreams are the disasters. They float on our emptiness. Their wings are voids of light, slices through the visible. They are insane, they make no sense.

They are a child gunned down by the protectors in 1.8 seconds. The car slid across the playground in the snow, and the untrained policemen were scared, because the void dreams were at work in their minds, evacuating sense into the possessions, which were themselves further sources of darkness, until the minds, souls, bodies, and feelings of the protectors were a single, seemingly continuous coil of fluid pain made normal.

Crack, and the boy was shot in the gut. He was bleeding on the ground, and the void dreams would not help him. He had a toy gun near his body, a ridiculous protection that boys use for self-possession.

His sister came to him, and the agents of possession pulled her off the boy's dying body. They pushed her to the ground and hurt her. They possessed her too, the protectors.

Where was the wind? It was cold that day, slick snow on the grass, and there was little wind, even though the lake washed near on the shore just blocks away. Where was the wind?

The cosmic politeness of it cannot encircle the disaster. There is nothing right in it. Even in daylight, the greyness has gone to black. We walk on the sidewalks with our eyes slit almost shut, trying to stay awake in the winter. The society is a disaster.

Maybe when you opened this book, you hoped that I would be describing the wind and reveling in it through language and through thoughts. Maybe we had a misunderstanding. It began so clear, like a day of sunlight on the snow with a royal, blue heaven cast about the outlines of frozen trees. It was easy as a walk through familiar streets and across the small, neighborhood park. There was almost no motion in the air, and you could hear yourself breathing.

But then things slowly changed, and then they began to move quickly. The turbulence was not just in the air, it was in the reality. A vacuum ahead of everything was drawing reality out, breaking it into shards as things aired and flew. Pretty soon, there was nothing stable, and the fluid was ever uneasy.

We came to a boy in a time and a place, a shard of the disaster of that time and place around the bright silhouette of the boy. The boy's loss was the vacuum, and the society's reality was sucked out in scraps into the void.

How can any of us relate when these things are normal?

*

To describe	O friend,
the wind is	O cold coasting night,
to avoid it.	O lost anatomy of a loss
My spiritual	Of safety.
exercise is	
to inscribe	O child,
it. The wind	Over and tossed to the void,
is an unruly	Only your own in a game.
inscription.	
What the	Oddity, O,
Stoics called	That is a silence.
the *kanōn*	

is nothing but a mark that slices the normal order of self-possession. This cutting is not violent, but is the void of force contained by the order of possession, a momentary suspension of violence. In the unconditional, there will be no violence. The wind rises in the moments when violence subsides and even its possibility seems unthinkable.

The wind stirs as suffering unfurls. I must sense suffering and move in it, become people again and not possessions. The mark of the disaster I call society is an ache I have forgotten in our head, chest, and limbs. The ache is always there, but I have avoided it, but then the wind has turned me to it for a moment, and I have a chance again to relate.

*

There can be no trust when there is suffering hidden in the structure of the society. The wind has to shake the structure apart, break it down. It must teeter and fall, for it is covering over the thing we need in order to relate. It is avoiding the suffering of people.

Now you might think that life is suffering. This is more of the avoidance that makes self-possession seem normal. Life has pain in it, but suffering is something else. Suffering is the denial of relationship.

The wind appears where relationship has been denied, and it rushes to re-open relationship. This is the process of airing things.

Suffering is the core power of the void. The wind must rush to it.

*

Here I am at 4:59 A.M. on December 21st, 2017. I am sitting in a chair that was left with this house by the previous inhabitants. The paint and wallpaper have begun to peel and patch off of the walls in this study. Antlers—the nickname of a vulnerable one sleeping in the next room—and I have begun to scrape them down. The walls are beautiful as they slowly reveal their history. Some day we will paint them again.

It is 5:03 A.M. and the light on the upright piano my mom gave us is soft and yellow, reflecting against the wall, the wood apron, and the dark veneer of the piano itself. I have a headache caused by either the wine we had last night or by the dryness of the Winter air inside this place. For even with a humidifier, the heating drains the place of moisture. I am getting over a cold, too, and perhaps my sinuses are partly stuffed up.

It's 5:06 A.M., and I am thinking of Tamir Rice. He was shot down twelve miles from here in November 2014. That was just three years ago, and the meaning of that single act cannot get through to the city of Cleveland. If it did, so many people would have to see that their daily life is predicated off of ignoring the bodies piling up in the poor and formerly red-lined parts of the city where racism made and makes its mark. People would have to come to terms with their callousness. It would fuck them up, oddly, to see how fucked up their life of possessions is.

5:10 A.M., and I am doubting this book, because it is so choppy. No matter what I do to smooth it out, make it plain, it draws back into itself and becomes a swirling jumble of sense. My outrage plays out in it as discomfort with a fixed system. I want the words to be fluid, even if they become opaque. I want the motion of their non-sense to find a deeper sense in my mind, for I know that the void of the cosmos is in us. It is our secret. It is the impossibility of possession.

5:13. 5:14. I cannot begin, no, I begin, but it is inadequate, to say what I think of this society. There are no words to express this emotion, it's a storm. To be in this society, I have to keep the storm on the other side of barriers, as if behind an industrial plate of glass on some spaceship designed for solar winds and atmospheric entries.

The storm would take apart the structure of my society. It would level it. In this fantasy, as the winds subside and the rubble of their world appears in light, people would appear alongside it, more free and whole than they have been in any time of my memory. They would be equals and would begin to relate. The vulnerability would be overwhelming, it would be unforced, it would be so open that there would be no need to focus on it. Instead, we would find what we want to do. We could be curious. This impossible fantasy is a joke.

I am trying to imagine its wish.

5:19.

Shaker Heights, Ohio, Summer 2017

The void

"Philosophy" is the name for a family of unsettling practices that were created almost three thousand years ago in an area between what is now Greece and Turkey, around the Aegean Sea. These practices involved new ways of considering the universe and one's society in terms open to all who could think.

Ancient philosophers came up with codes, exercises, and ways of talking to help them reason about how to live well. They didn't want to just listen to what authorities said. They wanted to understand why living one way, rather than another, was better, and they wanted the explanation to make sense to anyone who could think about it. They were the opposite of teachers who want us to memorize stuff and repeat it. They wanted everyone who did philosophy to understand why they live the way that they do. The philosophers also wanted us to get to the point that if we didn't have a good explanation for why we live the way that we do, it wouldn't be because we were just obeying someone else. It would be, instead, because things about life are unknown or unclear.

Philosophers experimented with living in new ways that arose from forming a relationship out of what truly makes sense, on reflection. What they created allowed them to live in a way that was aimed at being, relatively, autonomous. Philosophical practices were at heart disobedient.

*

And then one day, I took up the tradition of philosophy. It was a frigid, airy day. A bright, cloudless sky receded into the void of space. Since my collapse, I had been learning about the tradition. It was enjoyable to do in my rehabilitation time. I learned about some of its practices, and I read and thought about many of its theories along its almost three-thousand-year history.

I was working part-time in my local hardware store, an ACE. The people were nice to me and didn't ask many questions so long as I helped them with their queries about batteries that didn't work, caulk for windows, various kinds of weather seals, and even about a crock pot. My co-workers were all over the map of life—some past the age of retirement in a world without pensions, some young, some black, some white, and all with an eye for detail, which was nice.

At night, I would go home and read about philosophy. I figured that the best thing to do after leaving finance and its endless ruthlessness was to try on the most unpractical of things, or so I thought.

It turned out, though, that philosophy was practical, once you thought about it. None of us come into life knowing what we are supposed to do with our lives, and philosophy took up this question. It sought the point of living and had developed many ingenious theories and specific ideas about how to live well. Some of them were absurd, but the search for purposes worth having was about as practical as it gets. After all, there isn't anything to do if you don't have a purpose to your actions. Actions have goals.

Philosophy also made a point of going deep into self-knowledge, assuming that if we do not know ourselves, we cannot come up with a purpose to living that fits us. It turned out that self-knowledge is practical, too—so much so that I started to wonder about how people in my society use the word "practical" when there is so little emphasis on knowing ourselves in the midst of economic activity.

I never stopped to think much about myself all my years learning finance and working in a bank. I kept my mind on the wealth I could generate, my investment in my future wealth, and the competition and risks that surrounded everything I did at work and—it seemed—outside of it. I was always on the go, but going nowhere I had really thought about. Even absurdity would have been good for me.

Don't get me wrong. I did spend a lot of time thinking about who I wanted to be, but in a way that never stopped the world I was in. I took the images of my society and hung them around me, in my future. It was as if my future were an Instagram account, where I had "re-grammed" the shots of fashion models, stylish men I wished I were, and of restaurants, resorts, and homes on display. Marketing defined my future through my sense of who I took myself to be. I wanted to be a person made of the market. I felt self-possessed in it.

As I read philosophy, I found ways to circumvent the marketing and thereby my sense of self possessed by it. Philosophy has a way of returning everything to the void, as if a great, cosmic wind has swept up all of time and left you only with your relations, not your possessions. And who are you now?

By "relations," I mean the things that truly connect with you as a person and make sense to you, outside of any fear that you might have that, without them, you will be left behind in the competition of the world. Relations are not things on the way to a strategic victory, an out-competition; they are good in themselves so that you can trust in them to make life meaningful even when life is scary or rough. With relations, you let down your guard.

I started to see that all my relations in the void, so to speak, were the circumvention of myself, if that makes any sense. What I mean is that in the areas where I could trust, the unconditional areas, I was able to stop worrying about myself and trying to secure myself. Relations made me forget self-possession and its underlying insecurity. I was all right in them. Ironically, when I connected in trust with something or someone, I simultaneously become myself and got over myself, let myself go. I circumvented myself to find myself in the relation with others.

I loved this void quality of philosophy, its ability to make the things that I could not trust lose their allure and intimidation by showing them to be meaningless in themselves. Philoso-

phy had a way of loosening my entire society from its possessions, its locked-up insecurity and constant threat of violence or negligence. And wasn't the negligence—as people focused on securing themselves and left others to suffer, waste, or stagnate—as bad as or worse than a violence?

Still, as I came home and read philosophy, I started to realize that it suffered from its own limitations. It was categorically better than finance as a sensible way of living, but it tended to subsume everything into itself and become an entire world. This seemed odd to me, mainly because of what I had found through philosophy's capacity to void possessions and to make trusty-worthy things stand out. But I came to suspect that philosophy harbored a residual kind of self-possession in its way of absorbing everything into its world. Why did it do this?

As I looked more closely and thought more extensively, and as I began to read around, I started to contrast philosophy as a tradition of practices, ways of thinking, problems and theories or theoretical approaches with improvements in the ways people relate. Although philosophy helped void self-possession to make trustworthy relations stand out, it did not actually help with communication as much as I would like.

I noticed that I would find philosophy helpful to see what was going on in my life and to figure out an idea of how I should live, but it was not helpful in communicating with people. It had surprisingly little to offer in the way of good communication, except an admirable logic, rigor and—sometimes—clarity of argument. But living with people, communicating, being a person—these require more than analysis, argument or conceptualization.

They are more fluid than a justifiable idea of living well, too. I realized that philosophy is truly practical—more so than the finance I had pursued and the marketing I had absorbed— and it is, of course, powerfully theoretical. But it is not entirely relational. It can help us see our relations, but it does not teach us how to live with them. It can help us see community, but philosophy does not help us communicate.

I was being straight-forward reading the tradition and being honest with myself about the way it largely failed to be communicative. One thought I had is that the limitation I was seeing might be a philosophical problem that deserves more place in the tradition and that perhaps I was seeing how philosophy grows. But I didn't need to hold onto philosophy either. It, too, could fall into the void.

The second thought I had is that philosophy might be seen as a tradition of some three thousand years that is very helpful in many ways, but that one can put it to the side when one wants to communicate and to be a person with other people. I thought of this as growing up.

This train of thought, which I worked out slowly while stocking the shelves at ACE, led me to another one. What is thoughtfulness, once it is not owned by philosophy? I started sensing, and then imagining, a difference between thoughtfulness and thinking.

By "thinking," I meant what the tradition of philosophy has called "theory"—from a Greek word theōria, *which meant "to see," in the sense of being a spectator. As a common philosophical story goes, from the time of Plato, and especially through the schools of Aristotle that followed, philosophical thinking was primarily theoretical. It stood to the side of life and looked on dispassionately at the things as they are, seeing why they are and how they fit together in an order discernable by observation, inference, analysis, and deduction—to name a few of the many operations that went into the theoretical life. Theory aimed at truth, yes, but even more at truth involving a true explanation of what is true. Call that reality and its wider reality.*

The philosophical word for this wider reality in the Greek tradition was a logos, *a credible account. The word also meant the capacity to reason, and even speech itself, articulate language. It was many-dimensioned. A* logos *was a saying that was a knowing, and a knowing that could be said. The knowing, in turn, was an explaining, an explaining that was a thorough and penetrating seeing.* Logos *rested in* theōria.

What was knowing in theory? The story I read is that it was, at the minimum, a set of true beliefs and an explanation of why they are credible. True beliefs were explained as true by other true beliefs in a widening system of explanation that served, in the face of doubt, as a justification for the account in question. The point that interested me was that knowing was, at a very minimum, a matter of operating with and through true beliefs, related to each other. This interested me, because thoughtfulness seemed to me to work through trust, not belief.

As I read, I found that for the philosophical tradition, belief and knowing were tightly involved. And belief and seeing were, too. When you see something, you take it to be there, as a fact. That this was so was shown by how we reveal something we thought we saw as merely an illusion: we go and see that it was one. Seeing corrects seeing.

Furthermore, we often say that we have seen what someone was trying to say. Here, seeing became a metaphor for finding something to be true, in our minds. Seeing something mentally then implied finding it to be believable. To see, to believe, to know, at least initially, awaiting an explanation ... to draw reality close.

Thoughtfulness, however, seemed to be about relating, not laboring at accuracy and explanation. At first, I wondered, what if thoughtfulness is thinking made of relating? I did not mean by this that thinking would be made up entirely of relating, that it would be, quite simply, "made up," "make-believe." I meant rather that thinking would be made in part of relating. But what would this mean? It seemed like I was just adding things together, not seeing how thoughtfulness is a distinctive transformation of mindfulness.

Now, one day as I was punching the computer to record a purchase (the woman with the faux*-diamond studded glasses and tall, plush boots had handed me a bag with three keys she had duplicated in it), I realized that the sense privileged, literally and metaphorically, in relating is feeling—touch, and, by connotation, emotion. There was more, though, since relating is primarily interpersonal. As I considered it, even when we relate to something impersonal,* *we move back and forth by analogy and disanalogy with our personifications, appreciating the strangeness of, say, a mineral formation by the ways in which it exceeds our animation of it. The wonder, here, was in the strangeness appearing in the void of personification. Still the interpersonal had priority, a place of beginning from which we feel how things are in relation to us. Accordingly, to ask how thinking might be changed when joined with relating was to ask how thinking matters personally to us.*

Was thoughtfulness the personalization of thinking through the emotional and social life of belief? How do we feel about these things which we believe? What is it to live in touch with each other and with ourselves when we think? This sounded nice, but it wasn't exactly what I had initially sensed. It had, once again, been skewed back into theory. I kept orbiting belief and not focusing on trust.

Picking up shovels one day and stacking them against the wall near the linoleum-bright entranceway, I realized that I was interested in communication. Thoughtfulness, to me, wasn't simply "thinking+". It circumvented theory by speaking with people, first and foremost. It underlined the unconditional quality of trust in expressions of an invisible relationship. It was a way to form, not just see, our relations.

Being in touch, I thought, is about communication. And it is, so, basic to becoming a person. Without it, we can't relate to things as who we are. Thus, things never really make sense to us. We might think that something makes sense, but that sense is always abstract, because we do not let ourselves consider what it means to us in the intimacy of our lives. Philosophy, without being in touch, is always abstract. I knew this, untheoretically, and now I saw this, intimately.

Time to shake thinks up.

*

If airing things, if vulnerability, if relating, if all of them are a big mess, then the perspective of the void is the opposite. It is a stretch of relating, yes, but it is crystalline and clear, like sub-zero weather on snow covered ground at night—the sky infinitely remote, yet near in its ability to remove everything but the present. Freezing breath on freezing breath.

Part of being human is thinking about what is true, circumventing self-absorption by taking in the world and acknowledging our livable, or unlivable, reality. In such moments, things stand separate from each other, just as they are, both new and familiar at once.

The void's word for clarity is *delimitation*—"completely" (*de-*) at its "boundary" (*limitare*). It is worth noting that *liminal,* too, is related to *limit* as that which is at the threshold of an important demarcation—and yet crosses on both sides of it. The wind, in this figure of imagination, is the void's work of delimiting.

I think of the circumvention of wind circling around us and our situation, making things often uncomfortably present—*circumvention*, from "around" (*circum-*) and "come" (*ven-*) (*vent* is also the French word for wind, as in the English *ventilate*). To live around the wind is to have one's senses in it—also to be thrown back on oneself, seeing the world itself thrown back, tossed, twisted and settled.

In this stretch of text, I will focus on delimitation, and in the third stretch, "Figures of imagination" on circumvention. The two are related, I will often use the strange locution, "circumvention," but the wind is tricky and pushes that thought down along the way. We need a practical context to get the word to collect in plain sense.

Circumvention, it turns out, is where relating and being practical are joined, while delimitation is where relating and thinking are. Delimitation is the wind's word for thoughtfulness, and in this stretch of text, I want to discuss thoughtfulness.

*

In my effort to help free my sense of possessions, I am working on recovering a dynamic understanding of being a person. In the early middle of the 19th century, the German-speaking philosopher Karl Marx explored how capitalist production involved deepening forms of alienation—first, from the things people make in factories; then, from the craft by which artisans once made things in workshops; next, from collective control of our own working conditions; and ultimately, he thought, from what it is to be human. Factories alienated our production from our creative capacities and involved an order whereby people were dispossessed of their dignity while simultaneously being more or less owned by the factory managers, owners and politicians. By means of wage dependency on the miserable work of the factory, workers lost their distinctness as persons, not having political agency, creative time and capacity, or daily freedom. In capitalism, Marx thought, we are distorted versions of people.

The society of possession, including the ethics of self-possession, interrupts our being people, first and foremost through blocking the society of relations. The first stretch of this book's exercise with the *kanōn,* with the wind as an unruly rule of living, circled around and around this point, driven by the anxiety in my mind. I depart from Marx in seeing the distortion of the order of possession primarily in the interruption and blocking of moral relationships. The problem is not alienation from our practical life, primarily, but displacement, suppression, disruption, and replacement of our *relational* life with forms of manipulation and mere—strategic—objectification. In this way, Marx's diagnosis is actually part of the problem, for he maintains the focus on strategic power and practical realization *and largely disregards moral relationships.*

In an effort to delimit the dynamism of being a person, where the primary process is relational, **I am tracing out three forms of consideration in this book—relating (knowing by acquaintance), thinking (knowing about things), and doing (knowing how)—all from the primacy of relating**.

Knowing by acquaintance is the way we know people. Knowing a lot about people won't get us there—and nor will knowing how to manipulate someone. To know you as a familiar, we have to connect. What I know about you or know how to do around you may help (or it may hurt), but it is not enough. Relationships come apart precisely when the familiarity is lost.

Knowing about things is, at its most systematic, theoretical, even scientific. But it is also found in having well understood, true beliefs about everyday things. It is more or less objective in this way. The question is what it should become in relationships.

Finally, knowing how to do things is practical and can lead to agency. But can there be agency without relationships? Who is acting, a calculative stranger or a person, a familiar?

One way to address the problem of alienation in a society of possession is to restore relating to both doing and to thinking. in this stretch of my study, I focus on thinking as seen through relating, and in the last stretch, "Figures of imagination," I consider doing as relating. Relating, as we've seen, is open—all the way to the void in and around each of us. When thinking and doing are circumvented by relating, they become open themselves, not at work on possession, including self-possession. What is the quality of this openness?

The answer is simple, but has a lot of complexity and subtlety once you get past the first word. The answer is that **thinking and doing become personal**. The personal, far from being an indulgence, is the way of looking at ourselves where we are fully social, related to others, and dealing with the need for, and reality and deficits of love. For this reason, in the words of this text, it is the orientation where we begin aware of the void within us and of the void in others. Only in love is vulnerability open, and without vulnerability there cannot be love. The void speaks this in the language of this text, the language of, I'm calling it, wind. Thus the personal is elemental, the cosmos inside and outside us. This cosmos is animated by love, given to it by the way we are social in it and see everything in terms of the void appearing only once we are vulnerable.

With reference to thinking, the void also has a specific relevance: it underlines how thinking must be *delimited* by relating -- how thoughtfulness is a kind of delimitation in reverence or wonder whose underlying tonality is love. Delimitation, I think, is the work of being thoughtful, drawing on relationships. Thoughtfulness, I suppose, is thinking worked in and of relationships. So the point of focusing on the void is to focus on thoughtfulness as a distinctly delimited form of being a person, dynamically open through moral relationships and a personal relation to things.

What is it to be thoughtful? When I imagine thoughtfulness, I imagine *consideration*. Consideration seems to me to be different than simply thinking about things, because it delimits an intimate connection to the cosmos. The word has the word for a star in it (*-sider*). I see it as a way in which we take in our entire relation to something as from the void, thereby letting it delimit itself within the void as a star within the blackness of the cosmos. This is a poetic way of saying that in consideration we care about what we consider, personally.

In consideration, I open up just as the cosmos does, because my personal relation is at stake in what I consider. In reading my consideration, you read me as an open book. There is also *wonder* in consideration. I know that we wonder about things that are remarkable. Yet I cannot shake the sense that wonder is even more about *the familiar.* When I wonder about something, it is already a distant relative. The process of wondering shows that something is already near enough to be appreciated as something open and potent on its own, meaningful apart from me, yet something I care about personally enough to be drawn already to it ahead of myself. There, its independence from me involves my already relating to it, or trying to. In this way, wonder delimits—it delimits both my personal concern and the independent thing about which I wonder. We stand out in this void, silhouetted, so to speak. Wonder thus seems to reveal the way we are always related to things as separate from us yet open to us, if we can stop trying to possess them and instead respect them. (I even imagine, for a moment, that wonder could be in this way the source of accountability. Consideration, involving wonder, would then be a figure of accountability.)

It is an odd thing that in an order of accounting, where our wealth—or poverty—is made to prove itself—at least to the Board of Trustees and the shareholders—there is so little moral accountability to each other and to the planet. Perhaps a limit around which thoughtfulness is defined is that while we can think about anything we want—or try to—thoughtfulness has to be considerate. Why would this be so?

Because being a person involves relationships in which we must be accountable to each other, and the thoughtful is personal, we find moral accountability in thoughtfulness, namely, through consideration. That could be answer one. Answer two would be: **considera-**

tion, in involving wonder, is already morally accountable to whatever is both familiar and surprisingly separate from us. If an odd thing about the society of possession is that there is so little accountability, even in thinking's point and process, thoughtful consideration evens out. In this, too, it is like the wind.

I thereby delimit point one. Thoughtfulness is different than thinking in resting in moral accountability, primarily through wonder. Wonder, it appears, is the work of the void in thinking.

*

It is so cold these days. Erie, Pensylvania got four and a half feet of snow in less than two days. The temperature is in the single digits in Fahrenheit. Where I live, the snow settles into the ground, crisp to the point of grinding from dryness. You cannot go outside for long without thermal wear. To shovel the walk is to come back inside stiff and chilled to the bone.

Work is good and warm. And I have been reading. I try to be thoughtful. I spend time talking with people at work, both while I am working and for a moment on either end of the day. We all have to be on our way—the contractors, the home-owners, and we who work in the store—but it wouldn't be right if we didn't acknowledge each other and tarry.

When I was in finance, my bank sent me to Dubai one time. I had preconceptions. Based on what I had seen in travel and business magazines, I thought that Dubai would be capitalism intensified beyond anything I had ever seen. Part of this was true, at least in terms of seeing labor patterns and the ways that investment and marketing literally created a fantasy out of thin, dry air generating more investment! But part of it was not true at all though, because in the Arab Gulf, people stop to talk with each other—that is, so long as they consider you a moral equal.

You have to get me right on this one, or it will be misunderstood. In Dubai, there were many people who would not stop to talk with others because of the hierarchies and exclusions created by labor exploitation, rank, nationality, racism, and patriarchy. But the reason for ignoring others was not that capitalist calculation had outstripped relating. It was that relating was disfigured by old hierarchies—colonial and precolonial. What was remarkable, within a space of rough moral equality, was how people from the Gulf would stop to acknowledge each other and to tarry.

> *I found it especially thoughtful—this one thing, not the hierarchies. This one thing reminded me of a form of moral equality based on relationship, not self-possession and calculative strategies!*
>
> *It is odd that I had to fall apart to see the significance of this cultural practice, that, I fear, capitalism may one day erode. It is odd, but not so odd. The thing that was freaky about me was not my green hair and colorful beard; it was the extent to which I, inside myself,* ***was simply a strategy****, a strategy of fantasies from marketing and from a family life that had never interrupted my attraction to the order of possessions.* ***What was truly freaky about me before I broke down was that I had no moral accountability to others.*** *You could see it in my failure to take time to be with people—or with myself.*

*

What can we say of thought that is morally accountable to our relationships? This is a different kind of thinking than rarefied abstraction. It isn't simply "cognition." It is thinking that happens as a person in a circulation of interpersonal relationships and consideration of each other. We might simply say that **thoughtfulness is thinking in community**.

Someone who is thoughtful doesn't ignore people's suffering when becoming aware of it. Someone who is thoughtful doesn't ignore evil done to people when becoming aware of it. Aren't these basic delimitations for people?

A scene in a movie I love comes to mind. A wooden table in the country, outside, is set with lunch settings. But a strong wind is blowing, and the objects on the table teeter, fall, roll across the table as the wind moves in slow motion around them and through the leaves of the bushes and trees around the area.

This scene is part of a series of associations in which the narrator of the film comes to see that another world is possible beyond the suffering he and his loved ones experience in a world of war-time violence, totalitarianism, revolutionary killing and relentless deprivation. The wind along the table suggests that the form of the world passes away.

The norms we accept, often unreflectively, shape the context of our suffering. Self-possession, for instance, is seemingly so obvious and innocuous—the practical thing one ought to seek in a capitalist society built on colonialism, Capitalist and colonialist norms contain suffering and normalize it. They form the world as a scene of suffering and often as an evil that hides as what is well and right. "Take their land and ethnically cleanse them. They can do nothing about it." "Outcompete that guy. There will always be losers. Get as much as you can when you can."

When I am thoughtful, I want another world and want to see this world—the world of normalized suffering—scattered, and strewn on the forest floor. The normal should be cast to the void.

I love this iconoclastic thought, how considerate it is, how lovely in being deliberately abnormal.

I love this world-razing, utopian anger that is at bottom community.

When there is no moral accountability at deep points of a society, it is consideration to shake it apart unto the void.

Thinking then becomes a scene of accountability to the obviousness of what we hide from each other: our lack of relating.

Cognition becomes the counterpart to evil, rationalizer of suffering by virtue of its apparent indifference to its context of moral relationships.

For *here* we have a continuing city if we stopped seeking strategies for investment to come!

O what is a thought, a thought that is in this void?

*

As I have grown since my breakdown, my mother and I have grown more distant. Yet, when we speak, it is as if we are reaching each other in a way we never had before.

The distance is literal now living far from each other, seldom seeing each other. Before, it was hidden inside us. Something would make me speak to her, while I hid inside my head. Something would make her put on her make-up, while what she wanted to do was to run in the grass as a child.

We are distant now, but the distance is clear, outside us. This makes us stand out to each other, no longer trying to possess the distance, but letting it spread and grow.

I think that there is no hiding my failure to be normal, now. And, whatever her fear at the surface, this must make her feel, at some level, that her own suffering is valid. For she has suffered, trying to be normal. She raised me as a single mother. She struggled with depression and moments in which she seemed disassociated, losing touch with reality. She thought that she had to package herself, possess herself as a normal woman—made-up, beautiful, and with a man. But the tall grass swayed in her mind. I could feel it coming through her eyelids. Her world was elsewhere.

Now, when my mother and I speak, there is silence. In that silence, there is reaching. Its void is beautiful. The void, I say. (And I do not know why I am saying it, it came to me out of the void).

I came home one night and turned on my computer to watch something mindless and to forget. Although I am aware now and much more in touch with myself, I sometimes feel so much loss, and I feel so lost, that it is as if the sky itself would split apart in a confusion of unreality. It is as if there is no point to anything, and my entire life has been a waste.

In these moments, I do not know what it is that keeps me together enough to drift on them until I go to sleep. Perhaps it is just that under them I feel a current joy, strange as that sounds. I am alive and I am feeling all of this. The world actually means something to me. I find the open life all around me, even as it aches.

When I was a banker, I banked bucks and also nothing. I swirled around from win to win, plummeting toward a future when I would win even more. It did not mean anything, because the life right here, right now, wasn't sufficient.

The point of everything was empty—a fold-out in a magazine, a glimmering Instagram account.

I thought I owned my life, but it didn't mean anything presently to me. If someone had screwed me over on the job and made me have to give back my car, house, and life, I would have simply said it didn't matter, because the law of possession is to take the lives of others and possess oneself. My cynicism was ironically true, but it felt dull and affirmed the meaninglessness of my life and of the lives of others.

That, on a bad day. But not all the time. Not on the day I saw the family and could not do it anymore. Not on the day I cracked open.

I have been wondering what led me to do that—to do that supremely helpful, unhealthy, impractical thing that was actually a form of health!

One day, I came home tired and wanted to lose myself, because the loss was too great. I had wasted many years of my life. What did I do? I started looking around on the Internet and found an old movie from before I was born. Was that a waste, too?

The movie was made in the 1970s in and around Moscow. Its name was "Mirror." The movie was weird, but who was I to say?

It was snowing that night, thick, wet clumps that fell to the ground and covered the harder base that had begun to melt and freeze over. I remember looking out the window at my neighbor's backyard, lined by those warm festival lights on strings hung across space. Snow fell on them and melted, fell past them, and they winked.

The movie flickered pale white and gray-blue against the walls of my room, expanding from the computer screen on my lap like an intermittent portal on which my eyes were fixed. The movie made no sense. I fell asleep for part of it—I didn't know for how long from the plotless swirl of images, but later realized for just moments, several times. The film almost hypnotized me. I didn't know what it was, felt that it was often boring, yet I was gripped by its images time and again.

The images disturbed my sense of my own tedium and suggested to me as I only later realized that I was missing something. That night I dreamed. The dreams were chaotic and lifted on air. The society in them was severed by possibility, blown apart into fragments within which passageways formed that led somewhere that I hoped I might go. I felt only the feeling.

I kept meeting people I knew in the spaces, yet wearing differing outfits than I had ever seen, old outfits from another time, like buttoned up generals in a 19th-century waltz.

At one point, I woke up and saw my mother. She was staring at me without make-up, her eyes dull and barely open, yet inside them so dark that they absorbed all light from the world. Her hands were covered in cloth, an embroidered edge tactile and rough with tears and bits of loose thread.

I woke to this image and was hot, perspiring under my arms and across the backs of my hands. I felt my breathing fast, and I laughed out of nowhere about nothing until I caught myself and looked around. The computer had fallen by the side of where I slept, slouched like a bad cat against my body, and its screen was dark, the sole pulse of battery light beaconing out like a new form of cardiogram. I turned on the lamp by my bed and picked up my journal and a pencil. I wrote:

"I'm done with holding on to my life as if it were a possession. To say, this is 'my' life, is to say that I belong to it, like a lover for the one who is loved. If I could turn myself inside out, I would give only my insides to my outsides. I would be guts and bile, flowering vomit, wave on wave of illness."

Then I set down the pencil and laughed again, because it was 2 A.M., and I was surely in a half-awake delirium. This was right after the first time I saw the movie.

*

Fritz, it was never easy being your mom, because I never felt sure that I was being a good mom. This wasn't your fault, and I think you made things be about you, because it was easier to control them that way. If all you had to blame was yourself—your inadequacy—then there was something to be done. But if your mom was lost to herself, then what could you do? Your whole cosmos would be at risk by something beyond your control. Care itself would be compromised in your world.

I think you went into banking because it cohered with the feeling of instability inside you, making it seem normal, yet allowed you to control things, or so you thought. Ours is a world where people try to control things a lot. It makes me so, so sad.

I have not told you much about this, but as I think you have heard, I grew up with an alcoholic father. We do not talk about this enough—I do not. I have a hard time talking about it.

My father was in the Korean war. He never talked about it, but he had two scars from bayonet wounds, one on his rib cage, and another on his forearm on the same side. He married my mother when he returned, and after a few years, they had me.

It did not take long for him to drink so much my mother kicked him out of the house. He was a silent drinker, sitting like a crab at the bottom of the sea. But if you dislodged him—if he had to move to get something from outside or even to go to bed, he might lash out and turn into a fury. The wind would pour out of his mouth, and nothing would make sense of what he said. It scared my mother so much that she would tremble and shake.

Finally, one day, my father lost it completely and started smashing things. He smashed the framed photographs of his parents and my mother's parents. He smashed the front window so that cold air poured into the living room. He broke the old lamp with cream-colored, sculpted glass. It lay on its side on the floor, finger-tarnished bronze in a strange glow of the still lit bulb, while its cream-colored ruins glowed around it, a fallen halo.

My mother had had enough, and she kicked the drunk out. Huddling in the cold, he ranted at the house until the neighbors came out on their porches and stood back safe on their lawns, bundled up in pajamas, night gowns and wool hats. They looked nervous and as if they wanted to help.

The police took dad away. He spent a week in the hospital. Then, he left town, and we never heard from him again.

I was seven years old. It was 1962 in Euclid, Ohio not far from the lake.

I remember the winds that winter. They swirled around the house, strangely peaceful and safe. My mother would lock herself up in her room often after dinner while I did homework or watched TV. I never heard anything, but when she came out to put me to bed or to help me with work, her eyes would glitter and her face would be red and sagging toward the ground. She looked worn out. But her movements around the house were lighter and she moved more freely. She banged cupboard doors in the morning, no longer afraid to make noise.

I would often come up behind her when she was making my bag lunch and hug her, pressing my face into the slightly damp and rough texture of her bathrobe. It smelled like my mother, plain beneath with the scent of Ivory soap on top, and the slight mildew of the robe that was covered over by Tide.

Fritz, it was hard growing up. I feared men and was also drawn to them. I think I learned from my mother that I had to please them to keep myself safe. Yet I actually did not want to live with men. I needed them, or so I thought, but I did not actually want them.

Your biological father was one of those men, I am sorry to say. But in retrospect, I am still glad at life's ruses, because he helped make you. Fritz, you are the one man I have never had doubts about. If ever you thought I was judging you, it was my own confusion about how to bring you up.

When you were born, it was just you and me. As you know, I never married your biological father. I hardly knew him. You came from a night when I drank too much at the lounge where I would go once a week while you were with a sitter. Your father was handsome. The alcohol ran through me. My habitual antipathy changed to desire like a sudden rush of wind on a night when the weather doesn't know what it is doing.

We conceived you in the bathroom, I am sorry to say. But I hope you can laugh at its lack of glamor!

He left town the next day on his route. He sold new, synthetic siding to hardware stores and contractors. He lived in Illinois.

He came back to Cleveland several times over the next years, I heard, but he did not call me. He eventually changed jobs to work for RadioShack and was no longer on the route. I was too proud to force him to see you—and still too angry at men. I am sorry that things worked out this way, Fritz.

Life is vast, and it is funny how it works once you let it go. I so want you to let go of it, Fritz. You are such a lovely person. I have always admired your courage to be who you are, stubbornly sticking to your wild hair, even when your beard came out much wilder so that you looked like a villain from the comic books you read or that frenetic spirit from the 80s movie that you loved, the one about the couple who haunt their own house, taunted by a demon who will not let them be, the one who acts like a cowboy on fake ads on TV. You always loved this film, sitting there on the den floor half-way through elementary school. That was 1994, I think. You were my little and sunny punk.

I do not know why I am telling you these things now. I am rambling, too, I think! But I just wanted to write you. Fritz, I never cared if you made a lot of money or worked in a bank. I just wanted you to be safe. And I felt so much shame, sometimes, that you had to go through being teased and bullied and that you didn't have a father to help you figure out how things worked with boys. Men, as you know, scared me too, and so I would just sometimes be angry at life, for you, but also against your maleness.

Sometimes, I feel that life is suspended in a void, and that all we have are our relations. You are my relation, the one person I have tried to love truly in this world in addition to my mother. Do you know that? I am sorry, I am so sorry, if I have failed you in some lasting way. I am limited; it makes me so furious some times. But as you know, I keep things to myself and soldier on, like my barely known father in the trenches of Korea trying to possess a land for a war of global possession when none of it made any sense!

Your mom.

Heather Books

*

May 28th, 2017. NORTH PACIFIC OCEAN. *Associated Press.*

Hovering in a helicopter over the Great Pacific Trash Vortex that stretches farther than the eye can see in either direction, Arnold Thompson pointed to the plastics bundled together. Inside them were seal bones, the animal having been caught and died there in the tangle. "I can't imagine a worse fate than to be snared in other people's discarded possessions," Thomspon, a researcher in sociology at the University of Sydney, said.

Thompson and an international team of social and natural scientists acting on behalf of the United Nations Environmental Program (UNEP) are trying to determine the sources of the plastics, chemical sludge and other man-made refuse that fill the vortex, estimated by some to be the size of Texas. Caused by the ocean's natural currents, the vortex becomes a place where refuse dumped into the ocean gathers. Thompson explains that the vortex is a giant version of what happens when foam gathers in a river current's eddies.

"I don't think there's an easy answer," Mahinda Kawall, an environmental production engineer based in Manila and also part of the team, said. "We are talking about a planetary way of life, the form our entire civilization takes."

Researchers from the team have focused on three areas, the production of plastics, the poor regulation of chemical waste, and the patterns of consumerism that drive people to purchase and throw out products regularly.

"What are we going to tell our descendants when the way we live on the land has poisoned even the ocean?" said George Orland, an Environmental Studies professor and member of the Onondaga Nation working at the State University of New York's College of Environmental Science and Forestry. "We have thrown our planet to the wind while focusing on our possessions." Atmospheric and oceanic currents are interlinked.

*

I do something old fashioned that my grandmother used to do. I cut out newspaper clippings. Even when I read them online, I print some of them out and cut them around the edges. There is an area in the back of my small house that I am turning into a study. The wallpaper is the clippings. I coat them with a clear veneer that makes them fireproof and smooth on the wall. I have two of the six walls filled already, using my backlog of clippings, and am working on the third wall—basically, the entire nook across from the door where my reading chair and lamp sit. The other walls will take some time. They are larger, and I am looking forward to the room developing over the next years.

The clippings follow my unconscious interests. It is strange and beautiful, to me, even if it is a little weird, to see my focus over time. The Russian psychologist Vgotsky spoke of "zones of proximal development" to describe the way our growing often happens despite us in side-areas where we express an interest that we do not take to be central to our days. These clippings show my development in this way.

Lately, I have been clipping out news articles on waste. They are often short articles that fill up the side areas of online papers. They aren't announced with the spectacle of the latest 140 characters from my nation's president. Yet they are about long and cross-societal processes that show how we are actually living and what we are actually doing to our planet. Honestly, they strike me as clues to a wrong, even an evil.

It was actually these latest articles on waste that gave me the idea to line my reading area. Once I began, I went into my backlog of clippings. At first, it seemed random—to find articles from fifteen years ago on the ransacking of the museums of Baghdad next to a glamour piece about Miley Cyrus's meltdown around the time of "Wrecking Ball." There was an article on LeBron James crying on the floor of the court in Oakland in relief next to a story about changes in hedge fund regulation. I couldn't tell where my focus was.

But I had a system and I put up the earliest articles in the corner near the floor and then went left to right and up, until the first wall was filled. I then started on the left side of the bottom of the next wall and did the same. It established a chronology and allowed me to wonder about patterns when I was spacing out in my chair.

There were patterns. Mainly, I was preoccupied with the rules of games, their conception of success, and the way that they made losing necessary. These games could be sports games, but they could also be financial ones—or "games" of geopolitics that were filled with dismembered limbs and burned bodies. There was always waste in these games—the athletes torn up and let go, the ugly people excluded from the dramatic video, the melodrama where the destruction of relationships and harm to self were the plot engines, the traders pulling out their hair as their stocks fell, and the everyday people seeing their pensions and retirement investments evaporate into air. Then the eyeless dead.

By the time I got to my recent articles on waste, the pattern started to make sense. I was looking at a whole system that cycled around insecurity while it cycled around winners, possessions, euphoria, and losers, waste, hysterics, and killing.

It was sitting with these articles in my chair that I opened my mother's letter. I had told you that we have been distant yet closer than before. The letter attested to this. I read it without knowing what it said except that it was my mom opening up.

Then I began to cry.

As I cried, I felt my life turning over and over. It was as if I was rolling back to myself as I shed things that didn't matter, things I had put around me to distract me from the void inside me, the void I felt in my world which had entered my world as I grew up and taken over the house.

In a dream I once had, I was singing in the halls of an elaborate villa thinking nobody was there. But there were people upstairs listening and giggling. My silly singing made them happy.

But it didn't matter to the house. Later that night, I felt that there was a presence, something that would hurt me. I tried to tell the people of the house, distant relatives. They seemed cagey and dishonest, but reassured me.

As I decided things would be okay, I passed a room and a lightbulb exploded. I felt something there that would hurt me and that the people of the house were hiding.

Then the old mother of the house came out of the room and acted as if I were seeing things. But I could tell from her body language that she was going to hurt me too.

This was what my world was like, and as I cried, it came out of me and left.

*

To aim to be true as a person means at the least to be considerate. This, I suppose, is my thought in this stretch of wind. This concept of truthfulness makes no sense for people who think of accuracy as an amoral quality of good cognition. There was, not long ago, a philosopher who held that truthfulness involves sincerity and accuracy. But one can be sincerely evil. In the society of possessions, where to be dynamically human is split and divided into compartments that allow us to avoid our being people, it is supposed to be possible to be truthful while being evil. But who is being truthful here? Not a person fit for community.

A truthful cogitator is not a truthful person. To be a person, you have to consider other people as people too. The personal and the interpersonal encircle each other and intermingle. They are a limit that delimits what could possibly be a truthful person. If you fail to consider yourself or others as people, if you are impersonal or anti-personal, you avoid the truth of relationships. Thus, if you get caught up in self-possession or in trying to control others as if they were things you have to manipulate, you have failed to be a good person by being at bottom inconsiderate. You thus undermine the possibility of your being thoughtful through that relationship.

The figure of the wind is apt to interpersonal thoughtfulness, because the wind reveals the difference between the personal and the impersonal. We can use it that way, as a figure of imagination by which to keep the personal in view.

It's my personal *kanōn*. The wind doesn't care, but we do. The wind does not consider us, but we can. The wind does not make sense out of things, nor does it lose sense, it is.

But we stop making sense to make sense. Our lives are about meaning to the point that we avoid meaning if it brings us discomfort or anxiety. We delimit the wind, just as it delimits us. In its void, we stand clear, and it can do nothing but circumvent and avoid us.

The wind doesn't relate, but we do. The wind doesn't talk, but we talk—even in our sleep aloud to the emptiness, the open life.

And here, the society of possession sticks up its cognitive head and makes trouble again! According to an increasing wave of people now, simply to see another person as a person need not imply any consideration at all. A person can be a threat to your will and standing. To recognize that someone is a person is merely a cognitive designation. It may even be seeing a possible threat in the order of society. Isn't the society of possessions sophisticated to see "people" as an object-category? Two sticks, two legs, two limbs, two arms—and a fist.

A person? This is not what it is to recognize a person. Seeing someone as a person is part of relating personally to them.

It isn't, in the first, about practical problems of the will. That has already objectified the other person in a calculus of one's own actions. Nor is it simply seeing the person as a biological member of our kind, a psychological object or as a special kind of object in the world. This theoretical approach is thinking without thoughtfulness.

No, to relate to someone personally is to exercise the virtues of consideration—generosity, openness, sincerity, accuracy, accountability, compassion, and friendliness, to name a few. If you look at these virtues, you can see that they *contain* practical and theoretical considerations within them, *under the aspect of relationship.*

The problem with the diatribe about the insufficiency of personhood for moral consideration is its equivocation and question-begging. An abstracted concept of the person as an amoral being outside of relationships is assumed, quite different in meaning than people in interpersonal life relating. Then this concept is used to generate the conclusion that recognizing others as persons is as much a part of evil as it is a part of good. Did I say that the society of possessions becomes alienated in and by its own thinking?

The diatribe then backtracks to the interpersonal. Isn't cruelty an interpersonal relation? Isn't hatred? Isn't subjection?

Once again, equivocation intervenes, and the category of the relational slips through our hands. What you have now is a picture of points in space, "person" A and "person" B, and the things that go on between them are "interpersonal," *whatever* those things may be. Yeah, whatever.

But how am I relating to you as a person if I move you around and manipulate you for my ends without your consent or against your good? You have a life of your own. It is not mine to keep. In seeing you as a threat, I am not seeing you as a person with whom I can communicate; I am seeing you as a force.

Only you are not a force, and this is our problem. To recognize this is to undercut any use of the "interpersonal" to explain cruelty, domination and vice. The best we can do is point to a *failure* of the interpersonal, not its presence. What has happened if someone is cruel to me is that they have *suppressed* that I am a person and have instead treated me merely as a thing to be put down, set in place. They know this, too, because a large part of cruelty is showing someone who is a person that they have just been treated as if they were not a person.

But the wind is a figure of what will not be kept. It is impersonal, and as such, it can help us see who we are. At the same time, it is analogous to our freedom, for we will not be kept either.

The wind's powerful meaning is its power to unsettle everything in its path, leaving things stirred in the void. Similarly, **our meaning as people appears most powerfully in the void of a relation where we stand out unconditionally to each other. Then we see that we are complex and real, never just normal, and that**

to relate to each other is to stir everything in our path, unsettling our lives by virtue of each other.

To have a thought in the void is to consider people while considering anything. We are the ones who are thinking together, and to ignore this is to possess thinking as if it were not fundamentally a community relationship, inheritance of past people and legacy of future generations. Truly, to think without consideration is to misunderstand thinking itself.

So I wish this for you and your thought. I wish that the lives of people dispossess the order of theory until your thinking returns to its home in community.

Friend, I wish that people would stop turning people into possessions—cognitive or otherwise. ("I know what you are.")

Let's wish that truth itself were considered as considerate. Then we could not use "truth" to abuse people; nor could we use "truth" to avoid people. To assert a truth would be to ask people to consider the world *together*. Just as the wind relates us to each other, so would truth, then.

*

It is not easy to become a person, but the wind can help us coming from and returning to the void. Through a figure of imagination, an art of analogy, we can relate to the wind to show us the interpersonal and the personal.

In past work, I have called this art, "analogical implication"—the way we can relate to the elements and other forms of life analogically to show us something elemental or alive about ourselves. Then, what it is to respect ourselves is found through a figure of imagination that borrows from the cosmos around us. The cosmos around us thus informs the cosmos within. We are "rooted," "grounded," "flourishing," even "fluid." We compare our desire to "a strong wind." We become, in our minds, "a breath of Autumn's being" (a "West wind").

It is not easy to become a person, but the wind can help us. You must see, if it is not obvious by now, that in this stretch of a book, I am stretching, always, language. Here is not science but figuration. But figuration helps us be people by helping us relate to the world and to each other.

Science is not true without being personal. Making something of the wind is thus not inaccurate. It is *personal,* which means that it is a condition on the true.

There is more to truth than the facts. There are people who share their consideration of facts. And these people—we—need to find themselves—ourselves—in the cosmos in a way that makes personal sense.

So I have made something of the wind and of the void to bring out the personal conditions of sense, which includes the personal conditions of truth. I have asked the wind to help me circumvent possession and to delimit consideration. I have thrown truth to the void!

*

I am very alone now, but it is this solitude that allows me to relate. When I gamed my way through the order of possessions, ever investing myself in the prospects of further investment, I was always with people, even without a stable partner or my own family (my "own" family!). I dated online and had so much sex, but never intimacy. I was always emptying myself out in a tangle of relationship misunderstandings. I would not attach to people, but I surrounded myself with "them."

I loved to go out in Brooklyn or up and down Manhattan. I knew spots. I partied and partied, surrounded by partying people. They loved my hair and my beard. They loved my suits. They loved my money, and they loved the Something inside which I hid.

We possessed each other, but hardly knew each other. I never had a single, gentle talk my near decade in New York City. Mostly, we laughed—at each other and at the world. It was this laugh: "I own you, life." What would we be if not invulnerable? We were most invulnerable to each other.

I am very alone now, and this makes me happy. I don't want to make false friends. I don't want to lead people on. I want things to appear, crystalline and clear as a vision.

This sounds strange, but it feels right. As I have settled down, I often find myself seeing people just as they are. Since I do not want to use them, since I am no longer afraid of them, since I have been rejecting the society of possessions, and since I am exploring the way that I am related to others and to this life unconditionally, I see them as beautiful, strange, funny, even awesome, and generally—or should I say, uniquely?—as wondrous. They are beautiful being plainly who they are—complex, preoccupied, and mostly going on their way.

Of course, I am fantasizing still. The truth of them is stranger, but at least it is now personal.

There are some real shits, still. This is a society of possessions. The guys, especially, are hung up on themselves and insecure. But it is not easy to be a woman, either, without being insecure. The difference is how people relate to the constant insecurity of life in this society—or how they fail to relate to it, to say it better. The shits are not beautiful, and in their shittiness, I don't find them wonderful. I find them sad.

I feel wonder when I see someone living in insecurity as we all seemingly do, yet still treating other people as part of a community and being basically considerate! Life opens up around them, and their consideration seems to create a void in the society of possessions. Something about it even feels timeless, as if the time of the relentless profit has been broken and floats on air.

People do not know how to redouble loneliness. Loneliness is a void. In being lonely, I am vulnerable to my relations.

Loneliness is a condition of the relational. If I were never lonely, I would never be in touch. And if loneliness were not somehow fundamental to being a person, I wouldn't see the grace of another sharing time.

In the society of possession, we do not know how to redouble loneliness. It is a threat. Loneliness is a hallowed house with wind circling hollow about it. In my solitude, I can hear myself think, movement in that house echoing, the radiators steady and no longer making a sound, the snow outside heavy, the wind suddenly gone. 10 P.M. Time past work and before sleep. I can hear myself think.

The world is in a void, and our truths are at best ways to consider sharing it. Without letting the world stand out in its own way, I cannot see it clearly. Sure-sight benefits from being freed up to just see. Friends with intuition and observation, if I do not need to possess myself, if insecurity does not drive me to try to control others, if people are considered and the sense inside me trusts, then void-sight lays bare and open without threat that contains it or anxiety that would distract me.

Redoubled loneliness leads to seeing. A truth I can share appears in the void. All my relations in the void emerge because I respect them.

Black and white print of (color) "Antlers," 2017 by Misty Morrison

Figures of imagination

In a dream I had on New Year's Day, 2018, I arrived in a train station in Europe not unlike the Gare St. Lazare. People were coming out from the tracks, disappearing around me.

I thought,

in that city of a different hour,
    sea-lime settles on the scenes that laughter traces.

You should waddle in that violet hour,
        spanning storefront blocks,
        planning alleys of light and disappearance.

As you pass the mineral underbrush of clocks,
        grandfathers sedimented in the gardens,
        old fingers and ossified pigeons,

the perpetual sparks of sunfall
                          swansonged in the singing hour.

As you wandered through the streets,
        as you listened at windows, sing
        in these windows, speak
            in these parks.

First yellow captures the last hour's shaking.
        Orange rang through the rainyards and walks.
        Red shut talk inside our remembering

        while green,

            like sea light lost to the world

        runs through glass and vases
            trembles on the violet faces of trees
            upturned
                wondering love.

I dreamed of a nighting color, but I stayed asleep, bumping into people as I walked.

    I was trying to find my way out of the place. It wasn't a bad feeling, I wasn't trapped, but I felt mixed up and cycled about amid the busy rush.

At a corner, I turned to see down a hall and suddenly was in a field of tall grass. A woman was singing, her voice came out of my mouth.

If only I found a parting where

the cackle bird whimpers in the willows.
>That was the old, slow shallow—the land of smooth embraces.

At night, the crickets shake themselves apart.
>Wind and then laughing,

all come running,
>some high steps

shinning the tall grass.
>And ankles sang deep,

as all minds inscribed
>the momentary silence of clouds.

All night, everyone is blended,
sweat ribs hum, track of fingers, ache
in local, holding motion.
>Pulse lights in firefly fields

wink.
>Brother, run your fingers through your hair and think.

Fall wind follows through the leaves,
>leaves behind voices.

I was speechless when she stopped singing from me. I was confused, but it is like this in the firmament of our minds. The cosmos rolls upside down beneath our lids. Poetry is the automatic tickling of the animal we call "human." It is, quite literally, the autonomy.

Where the hell was I? I felt air gusting through the hall as if a subway had arrived or a door to the street had been propped open. But the dream continued on, down a corridor into a metro stop.

There were fewer people by the line, waiting. The sound of a car far off fading down the tracks rang along the tiles until it was a memory of a hum.

An androgynous person was singing quietly beside me, a song in Arabic, simple and modulated in tones I could not imitate due to my limited range. It was the night of singing!

It was so cold at the station.

But I could feel how

My mind cracked open and I was back in
            our home is a house of reflections.

                          See the
cloudbank in the table,
        the translucency of glass.

Windows cross through objections,
    and daybreak scatters space
                                on
blank walls winding,
    willing in the sock soft hush of shadow.

See at the brink of the back door:
    my father with his full beard.

    (Hear around on oblique angle:
        the cat's feet cuffing on carpet.)
Elsewhere, the winter swindles images
    of lavender-white
escarolls
    of plastic:
Talk of a tractor broken by a gut bare trailer box.
    It shelters sight   from frost stripped fields
                          swirling in the given sun.
In late evening, orange runs over its face,
    kindles its loss,

    and once,

the fire bare twilit hearth in the sifted heart of nightfall
played stillness for the hour both cold and warm,

    running through everything,

    all like motion...

As we circle past fenceposts and branches,
        the shoulder of your roof crosses my roof,
one limit above our second story light.
        Now hear the purple airing rushed with night

Inside the shower, I dried off my arms,
        shivered half a century for my song to talk.

I could see the subway and the person singing Arabic. Had they sung me that song?

    There had to be a way to stop the dream. I felt that if I reached above ground again, I would break into splinters of light and find extinction.

    I felt many things, but now the tunnel had become a wide, open square across which a single walkway wrapped in glass spanned a mile of the city. The city was no longer Paris, or New York, of wherever it was that I had been. No, it was Budapest, or something like it.

    Someone passed me with missing teeth and smiled. *I—and no one else—*sang,

                                Somewhere,

        while you are sleeping, gulls suspend
      the sea's awake.
    of waters, dawn.
    of anything, hominid.

       Roll through your side,
           mutter. Eyes
dart   skies
           beneath
           your lids.

Verbs enjoy the archaic
language no one knows,
           and rise
         and dive
          as surf.

It was a show tune, a ballad, coming out of my mouth! The person without teeth was smiling so wide their mouth was a tunnel of air.

    The wind now picked up along the square, and as I turned around, I found myself in a forest. This sound of forest was like a sea's roar. I was ecstatic and started running through the brush. It was getting dark. I was joyous, no, I was euphoric. There was wisdom in the smell of soil and in the damp, rotting wood of the stretch.

    I had made it back to myself by losing all sense of direction, and there was nowhere else to go. I was muttering the words of people I had never met. It was as if a society had decided to possess me.

One last time, I sang, this time a spiritual,

wash of cars along the lake's blue shoulder,
Sunday, someday, as a card
    that chances streets, a place to eat.

Look in, look in, asleep and attract,
    abound
      in slow form, my friend.

*

Figures of imagination, only when you let them come to you, only when you ride them out, are you able to find that they are, strangely, practical—they bring you to where what you do relates to you. So practical, that is, only if you began by relating through them. They are practical only if you are at first vulnerable and open to the void they carry, coming from nothing, touching nonsense, rushing on to something that stirs you when you wake, a memory of the outside that you cannot truthfully shake.

Dreams are among the things that are vulnerable. You can't control them. They happen to you. This makes dreaming in public problematic. I have found that to be vulnerable is often to suck out the fear between people, as if vulnerability were a void. As the fear leaves, it shows up—as fear or as cruelty. People get angry and afraid, because the fear is leaving them. Their fear may even translate into cruelty. They re-experience fear coming up as they experienced it going down inside them. Just as wind scatters the leaves outside in a wild and circular mess, so vulnerability causes fear to break free of bodies and to fly about the room until people—good people, at least—recover themselves, like scraps clustered in a corner around an invisible and departed core. And then, stepping through it is a shaken one.

Is to dream in the open to attract the fear that is being possessed and contained? Wouldn't it be more prudent to keep our dreaming to ourselves? Wouldn't it be better to form an argument and to engage the stressed-out world through people's beliefs and calculations?

I can see how that could be. Dreams aren't wishes. They move sideways away from the directness of fulfillment. They do not ask; they decenter. The medium of the dream is confusion, not expectation. When dreams create expectation, they do so by confusing things first, clipping and cutting, mixing, recombining. It takes an entire relationship—to the one dreaming and to oneself—to have a sense of someone's dream. It requires knowing someone, singular and familiar. Time and intuition. These are not things that can be generalized, calculated, argued. You can't know people in general, only one by one—

But the world goes fast and self-interestedly. If you do not possess yourself in it, you will be lost. In such a society, dreaming, though, is messy, vague, irrational. It doesn't get you anything since you are passive to it, and it doesn't make sense, at least not as a way to figure something out deliberately for some reason. Dreams don't begin with a purpose and then calculate how to obtain it. They cast about and work out a nest of association. Dreams don't figure out what to believe—they make things up out of nowhere, recombined scraps of the day in the night's vision. To let your dreams out in the open is to be a practical and a thinking mess, waking error of calculation and cognation. You present as unselfpossessed, as unmade by the dream. It's a vulnerable position to be in, especially if you are subject to the myriad oppressions and power inequalities that structure the order of possessions and its colonial history in capitalism. The fear released in dreaming out loud is the loss of control in a society where you must be in control to feel safe.

What to make of our vulnerability? What to make of dreaming? Or rather, how might we become practical within our vulnerability and thoughtful within our dreaming? How might we understand better the practical wisdom dreaming in public might have to teach us?

To answer these questions, we have to turn to relationships.

*

But how can we be *practical* when we begin with relationships? In the society of possession, being practical is *the* self-possession. Self-possession is possible through putting being practical first. *Be practical!* It is the hardest core of the oppressive reality of the society of possessions, the thing that must be broken last, because it is first. If you were to put relationship first, you would be open. If you put thinking first, you would be passive. You must put being practical first to defend and protect yourself,

Everything changes if you begin with relationship, that is, with a personal approach to people and to things. Then you must consider people, that is, be thoughtful. What is it to be practical then?

then to own yourself against possible threats to your control.

This is why I have ended my study with it. It's the hardest part to erode in the wind.

When you are practical, thinking comes *in the service* of the practical, just as science serves industry and the military. "What can you do with that [course of study]?" is the voice of the practical.

Relating then comes after the fact of industry—to provide relief from the relentlessness of self-possession or the tedium of thinking done for ultimately calculative purposes. "We've been practical all week—let's take a vacation, see a movie, hang out as friends!"

O, the practical! In movies that haunt my society, aliens from other planets come to Earth, and what is their intent? The military is usually the first to meet them as the organized expression of society. Most of the films center on a viewpoint involving the military, even if a civilian point of view holds out the hope of a relationship. Using the military, the default response of the society of possession is to address the arrival of the alien as a likely threat that must be turned into a beneficial calculus or eliminated from the Earth.

Science is used by the military to figure out what the aliens are and how to handle them. The thinkers serve the fighters. Strangely, as if in a dream, the films also seem to understand that this is the wrong approach. The civilian point of view—or the character of a rogue scientist—provide the hope of a relationship with the aliens, which is what is wanted to satisfy the fear of the insecure armies.

These films display the priorities of the society of possession. Is there a memory of colonialism here? If you come uninvited into our lands, is it because you want to take them, enslave us, or kill us off?

Who is the alien? The void that we cannot avoid is in us.

*

In the society of self-possession, being practical is commonly thought of as being calculative and effective in achieving the things that you want. You must keep yourself together and get things done, finessing and forcing, twisting and lightening, connecting and excluding until the aims of your intentions are reached.

There are many ways that we process things, but a society of possession privileges only one—and to such an extent that it tries to suppress moral relations. The one privileged is the practice of possession, which at the limit voids relation. It is violence. Possession is called "practical."

The privileged part of our dynamic humanity is then our way of knowing how to do stuff to get stuff—and to keep it. We must protect it from all the others. This becomes normal, although it is selfish. It becomes self-possession.

But people are dynamic. At their most cosmic source inside themselves, people who want to be people begin by relating, because without relation nothing makes personal sense, not even the practical and not even what we know about life. If we are not open to something, it can't make personal

The practical ones have the reality of deeds. They cause things to happen. They live in the mastery of effects, in the reaction by which unintended effects become redirected ones. To use a figure from basketball, the practical ones own the court.

But there is a different sense of the practical that appears rising on the wind, once one starts to move with the wind as an unruly rule of living. I want to explore this sense of the practical—**a being-practical that moves through a being-relational.** It is a sense of the practical that cannot be divorced from the moral, for I believe that one of the severest grabs of the society of possession is the grabbing of the practical away from the moral, as if truly practical people do not have time to be good people. No, no, they get to calculate when it is good to be good, as if such things are optional.

*

It is not that in relationships there aren't things we should or shouldn't do, customs we would do well to respect, forms of desire that are loving as opposed to forms which do not belong in relationship. *It is that in relationship, the openness of the person is first given as a destabilization of anything practical or theoretical, not immediately and all at once, but across the movement of the relating, pulverizing assumptions and intentions as the meaning of the singularity of the person opens up.* In this way, relationship begins in the void, not in sense to us. When things are personal, we are in it with them, even as there are things to do and to know. Relating is the origin of autonomy, where we can be open in a world that makes sense to us.

Being open, relating is unavoidably vulnerable. Since we have to open ourselves to life for it to mean anything, in opening ourselves up, we have already lost our self-possession. There is no way to avoid the void that we are and that appears when we relate.

When my mother died, I had been working at the hardware store for a decade, and I was in the early stages of middle age. I had begun going to school at night to study accounting. I found that I wanted to use my knowledge of finance to work against the corruption of finance, and I made an oath to myself to be an accountant who would serve the public interest.

I was at work the day I received the call that she had died. I was stacking drip catches in the back section where you buy stuff for gutters. I turn off my phone at work, but Tahinda called me from the front and said that a call had come through for me on the store line. My mother had died in her sleep while watching a film in the social area of the assisted living / condo complex where she lived. I asked which film. "Birdman" the man said. She had fallen asleep to it and never awoke.

the presumption of objects—even if there is no way to arrive, "thrown" into a relationship outside of a practical context and a set of assumed beliefs.

We are practical beings who seek to understand things—there is no problem with this. But we are also relational beings who seek to connect. The problem is when connecting becomes subsumed ahead of time in what is known or in trying to make it become known, without mystery—or when connecting is subjected to things we are supposed to get out of it, as something that is simply to be done, without the perpetual frustration (and gift) of getting nothing out of a relationship—not even complacency—but simply relating instead, having nothing that is to be done in relationship, but simply being in it.

Thus, I am often alienated by relationship and disturbed, vulnerable. It is a good thing—I am unhanded and my mind is opened.

*

What if we began this way, circumventing self-ownership: to be relational is the first way to be practical *as a person*? This would imply that people who put calculation first are somehow not acting as people, even though they have the

The cause of death was heart failure. She was 72 years old. She had never had heart problems before. Apparently, her heart just gave out. Since we did not know her father's genetic history, it is possible that there was an explanation on his side of the family. My grandmother died of cancer and had a strong heart.

My mom and I talked a lot over the decade following my breakdown and my reconstruction. She was a lovely woman, especially when she told me what she was dealing with inside. It made sense, and that made it easier for me to forgive her and to relate.

I kept reading philosophy for about five years. Eventually, it became tedious to me, but I sometimes still pick up the dialogues, letters or treatises of ancient philosophers. I find it gives me faith to think of them so earnestly seeking wisdom, and I find it funny when I think of the big theories of today that are part of the production of knowledge but which lack the simple gesture of living. I'm sure someday I will go back to philosophy, when I am looking back at life.

I found myself appreciating much more community discussions. A couple years before I stopped reading philosophy regularly, I started going to a local discussion group about moral issues. There were many different kinds of people there –old, young, professionals, students, the unemployed, the retired, and people of different cultures and religions. I loved hearing everyday people think. I found it practical.

potential to be people. This sounds strange.

The personal, however, is not about getting things done. It is not about knowing things. It is about being, in particular, being connected. This is what dreams are being despite ourselves, when we have stopped acting and stopped thinking in a logical and deliberate way.

Dreams are the void of a connection where the world makes sense to us as people, allowing us to be in it.

When we wake, we are closer to ourselves or jarred from the practical order that relentlessly summons us when we are thrown into daily tasks at the sound of the bedside alarm.

You have to read differently to read in relationship. Things come up and go. You have to tarry. Correspondence and tarrying are non-identical twins, but their correspondence does not create their correspondences, and their tarrying does not do work.

140

*

The point of the practical is to determine our actions, seeking what we take to be good to us and figuring out the ways to obtain or enact it. But what is good to us? We cannot know unless we relate to life. And who is that, "us," "you," "me"? We have the potential to be people—even if we do not treat ourselves as such, or treat others as such. We have the potential to be soulful—even if we do not see ourselves as such, or treat others as having little that matters in their souls. We have the potential to find ways to make sense of things—even if we do not see how we do this or treat others as if they don't know how to, too.

We see people all the time, but we may not treat people as such. We are people, but we may not treat ourselves as such. For the most part, we make choices to follow and to enact what makes sense to us in our souls, personally, and when we don't, we can be haunted by the choice later, having betrayed or missed being true to ourselves.

Recently, as I wrote in "The void," it has become common to point out: but the abusers, the patriarchs, the racists and the cruel—to name some of the most vicious things people can become—see the abused, women, the race oppressed, and the humiliated *as people!* This is precisely *why* they abuse, put down, discriminate against, and torture people. Others being people is threatening.

But this is not to treat others *as* people, to relate to them as such. It is to see people as threatening and to relate to them *as problems* in an effort to cover over and possess their personality and personhood. The vicious idea is to make using people part of simply being a person, as if that is a given and not an achievement. But when you manipulate people practically, having this intention lead the way ahead of relating, you are not treating them as people, because you are not paying attention to how things rest in their souls, how they consider things making sense, and what they have chosen or want. And in doing this you are being immoral, because you do not treat people the same and as people everywhere. You simply try to contain them. (And look. A racist idea—it gives you a false sense of containing some of us.) But the basic principle of morality is to treat all potential people *as* people, all the time—holding them accountable or being with them.

This is not some pious wish or liberal fantasy. It is the only embodied truth for people who have not closed off themselves. The militants who reject it are themselves struggling with the violence of the society they understandably oppose.

The point is this. To be practical is to set out our actions, the actions of people, as these make sense to us personally. If you aim to do something that doesn't make sense to you, not at all, not even with some higher justification that you trust, then you are not being practical. And if you aim to do something that implicitly holds or explicitly treats others *or even you* as an object or as a commodity, rather than as a person, you aren't being practical, not you, the person. To be a person and to connect with things personally takes being in relationship with yourself and with other people. You have to start with relating, with simply being-with. In this way, relating is the first practical thing for a person.

> **It comes in the breath of kissing. You must soak up the warmth from those lips, because they are relating only in that emptiness that they eat from out of your lips.**

*

Okay! Okay. The first virtue of the practical according to the wind is *circumvention*—at its heart, a dream-like process of relating, a multiple way that defies any agent's calculus of purpose. "Circumvention" is also the name for practical wisdom when that wisdom must begin with relating.

Let me be clear about what we are dealing with here in the "practical": not simply what action theorists call *teleology,* the aiming for ends by an agent with purposes in mind. Rather, we are dealing with acting *as a person with other people in a space that is opened, at least in its being, as community—or at the very least a community's possibility.*

To be practical as a person is to be in community, at least as a possibility you work from and to, beginning with the ways you relate to other people and persona (for the more than human world is personified in our more than human relations, fellow living ones, land that is kin!).

The "doing" here of the practical is a doing in a world with others, a doing together or apart, but always *related,* even if in the void of unconditional consideration of the self-determination of others, themselves mindful and related with you in the void. The practical is in this way in the space of "we" before "I," "you," or "they."

The question I have for the wind is how being practical in and *as* community appears, since in the society of possession, I have been trained to think of the practical as *separable* from the consideration of people and of community. "Be practical!" is often a rhetorical strongarm for "stop being moral, stop thinking of others, stop being in community."

Here is where dream-like and relational circumvention comes in. The idea behind circumvention is simple. Think of bare teleology, bare practical being, as a search for means for ends, an intelligent push to realize our goals. Like a robot—which comes from a Czech word, *robota,* for "forced labor"—bare teleology gets shit done, pushing as directly as it can toward its goal.

---

measure seeps through my protections. So, too, I am in a state whenever I get home from work.

To develop a relationship with the void where the void appears only in disappearance is to develop a relationship with life in which the underside of its coming is its going. Rousseau called it a sentiment of one's own existence, but it was not until Jean-Luc Nancy that the "one's own" was revealed to be a refuge of denial. Existence is never owned. It is mine (French, "propre"), only because I relate in it. "Mine" is the bare fact of my relating, that I am given in the relating. "You are mine" means "I am yours."

Life when it comes is already going. It swells and fades, ends—then arrives.

In summer, I soak in this freeness to resist the absolutes, the masters, and the injustice—to protect vulnerability.

Of course, this is exaggerated, since a goal might be such that it demands that we are restrained and speculative (for example, if the goal were to observe the stars). But the point is, teleology says nothing about the *kind of agent* that is in it. It could be a robot, a corporation, a computer program that is along some spectrum of artificial intelligence—or a fairly normal individual in the society of possession trying to possess themselves through the market by being selfish and competitive.

In other words, the *agent* need not be *personal*. But as thoughtful people, we can't plow through things in life disregarding people. As thoughtful and vulnerable people, we live in a world with others and we have to relate to ourselves, too, to stay open and free. Moreover, as related people open to the void, the world of life is our relative. We can't just plow through things on this planet to get our goals *if* we are going to be considerate and vulnerable. Rather, being people first, we must act *interpersonally*.

Circumvention means to tribute that. This point is not merely one of emphasis or restraint. It goes deeper. Relationship is, at the least, two-wise, not mono-directional. Contrast-

It is summer, the most vulnerable time. Bizarrely, time overflows even in the midst of a violent society. Warmth with no

ing with teleology's mono-directionality toward the goal, vanquishing or strategizing its way past all obstacles, relationship is *multi-way.*

Teleology goes from the agent to its ends, pushing on. The ends are not of the same kind as the agent. They do not communicate with the agent as party to the process, as person (in the void) who cannot be possessed and who has a life of their own. Ends are simply things to be realized.

But not so with relation. In a relationship, *I* may initiate, but nothing happens in a relationship—no relationships takes place—unless *you* also participate, unless you have a mind and will of your own.

And it is not just you and I; it is *many. We* need to be, to be in relationship—at least as a possibility. If you and I close the world out, casting "them" as obstacles, we have become a joint agent plowing through the world as if people were obstacles or means to our ends. We cannot close others out if we want to relate.

And this changes everything, because being practical can no longer simply mean getting shit done. Once the way we are is interpersonal, doing has to mean at the very first finding the point where *we* begin, or, in disagreement, where we are in question. It has to start with

communication, the multiple way to the multiple that is open community.

Here is an ontological difference that carries moral weight. We're not talking about simply a kinder, gentler teleology when we speak of "circumvention." We're talking about a revolution away from hardness and toward vulnerability, away from selfishness and toward multi-wise consideration, away from beat-down cogitation and toward thoughtful working through of disagreement, and away from stick figures using sticks and toward a community of people who will not avoid the voids in life.

So why "circumvention," then? It can't be because it could sound manipulative and clever. That would make of others more things to be outmaneuvered on your way to realize your ends. Circumvention does not imply sophisticated avoidance and manipulation, please hear that. "Circumvention" is a word that means to come around, rather than to go through. Coincidentally, it seems to contain the word

Like the cukes, hot peppers, tomatoes, basil, dill, varieties of thyme, lemon balm, mint, oregano, chamomile, lavender, chives, garlic, tamarisk, boxwood, peonies, black-eyed susans, spurge, clovers, sedum, hens and chicks, varieties of tall grass, blackberries, day lilies, clematis, junipers, sandcherry, bird's foot tree-foil, and the baneful bishop's weed and english ivy

for "wind" in Latin, *ventus*, although its root is from the Latin *venire* (to come). Circumvention—in the way it is stretching here in the wind—is the process of seeking to find how *we* could be relating in our agential life, making way for each other and fellow people, circulating (*circum* is from the root behind "circle," the round) in community.

The "around" suggested by the word means detouring when we would otherwise plow through people or see them as merely obstacles in our way to be removed. It also means imagining the round of community, the way "we" would have to position ourselves in order to face each other if we were to each be able to see each other in a community of more than a few (we would have to be in a round, or one of us would be cornered off from view from another).

Circumvention is the wisdom of holding a gathering, prompting a relation and rolling, twisting, working, spacing, withholding, waiting, turning, talking and being through it. Circumvention is in this way also the way of working *around* the society of possession for a community that is already here and is still *to come.*

Circumvention, as I imagine it, has many of the qualities of the wind and follows well the wind's unruly rule of living. Wind is fluid, without "fixed shape," flowing—it seeks its way through to relate. It goes around things, too, following on open space, being in passageways, sifting and awakening, but also seeking the level in calm. Wind opens us to the outside and is there to us only in our being awakened to it, relating through it.

Yet the wind is independent of us, vaster and more "other" than our imagination. In its impersonality, it cannot be a mere extension of our wills—and so, too, with all other people, who cease to *be* people in our eyes and in our behavior if ever we treat them as mere extensions of our wills.

Morphing like wind, then, circumvention finds the open space *between* people, because *there* is where a multi-wise relation begins. At this point, circumvention finds a point that is the most paradoxical for the society of possession's view of the practical as teleology. Circumvention finds *disagree-*

The things that disrupt your con-construction, leaving you speechless and without a thought, a thing that avoids explanation by a construction of a construction. Otherwise—it is not a concept moving. No, that thing loses its meaning setting, books, but their arrangement on a table around, however, candles, flowers, wind, breaking ... their construction ...

ment, as the wind finds the void in the normal presumption of shared norms between people. Circumvention, far from fleeing disagreement, *opens up* disagreement—holding it in circulation, as one holds a gathering, a promise, or a person in a constant, low hum of movement and adjustment!

Disagreement between people is the way in which we can be real with each other and work through conflict. Why? It is the way *we* appear as a question and as a possibility. Circumvention does not deny disagreement, pushing past or over it, but accepts it as the way to community. Disagreement is the place between people where the multi-wise ontology of relating appears *as such*. There, the calculus of teleology must be cast to the void if one is to relate. Anyone who does not stop what they are doing in a disagreement and work through the conflict must turn others into obstacles and cease acting as a person. *Sí!*

...

Time out. Let's pause and think about what circumvention implies for being practical:

(1) Being practical becomes being interpersonal, first, in multi-way relations decentering the agent.

(2) Being interpersonal means holding open disagreement.

The way of disagreement is the way to the interpersonal, and the way of the interpersonal is the way of the practical—says the wind. Can *we* hold this double vulnerability?
...

What, though, to be clearer, is disagreement? From the standpoint of the *kanōn*, it is more than differing over facts. The issue is not *what* people disagree about, but *how* people are with each other. In disagreement, people have become caught up in possession. The disagreement is to make this clear.

Disagreement is on the side of the void at the moment when self-possession is faced with dispossession by the dispossessed. *Consider us. Give us our due. Stop oppressing us. Let us be self-determining and free as you wish for yourself. Get off our backs. See us. Stop using us. Do not abuse us.* And the same for a single person demanding, *respect me.*

Thus, the cause of disagreement, if we had to make it essential, is <u>not</u> finding the void in each other, and the consequence of disagreement, again stating the matter essentially, is bringing the void out between us *and* in each one of us.

Disagreement might be said to be the call and the demand to make self-possession disappear.

Disagreement might be said to be the sense of the void when acting in community.

Disagreement might be said to be the practical when the relational is first and when community is first reached through holding open the space between us, rather than plowing through any one of us.

...

Circumvention *loves* disagreement! Let's turn a primarily calculative situation into one where people matter first! Disagreement breaks open the lock and the wall. It cracks the shell. It reveals.

The pragmatism of possession suddenly appears hollow and untrue. *You are losing people, losing yourself as a person, when you stick to your calculations and ignore disagreement. It is heart-breaking, because you then lose the possible depth of growing as a person and the meaning of time in community. You lose others and the confidence of others in your heart.*

...

How does that feel? "It feels weird, awful, and alive." So says the normal in self-possession. "But the vulnerable, the people? I feel that we could possibly work through the problem between each other to allow us to become free together, to allow and to let go of the conditions have structured the manipulations that 'society' on top of us. I feel that I could stop my cycling of abuse, my ever compromise and self-compromise in the society of possessions. But vulnerability is so terrifying."

Remember, the wind is like movement where things appear out of nothing— blurring, disorienting, then showing up, clearing the surroundings so that everything there spins ... In its relating, everything is in touch with everything else, our intuitions open. ... And so, too, with circumvention when it holds disagreement open. The frame of our self-possessed world breaks, the outside is in, and we are in our nervous systems electrified as we come to terms with our vulnerability *with* others. The multi-wise relation begins.

But please, reader, note what we are not discussing. If in circumvention's disagreement, all people in the disagreement are to be people with each other, the electricity of the moment is not one of threat, unless it is threat disappearing as a memory of the abuse we carry inside us, rising upwards to the void. In the wind, we are vulnerable with. Your disagreement that broke open my walled self-possession demanding that I see you flows back on and in you, too, not simply reverting to more strategy and calculation, more objectification of me as an obstacle in the way of your tragically and self-contradictorily impersonal teleology. Disagreement involves us both in vulnerability.

...

Circumvention circles and swirls in this wind, this alley of light and disappearance. Like a dream, circumvention finds the

Still, wind makes things *dis*appear. Wind finds the void. Its friend is "virgin" "as void as [X] was when [X] was not yet" (Reiner Schürmann as Meister Eckhart). What does circumvention, analogously, make disappear in disagreement? Not *each other,* but *the society of possessions* that keeps us from seeing the void between us in which we can relate unconditionally.

Circumvention makes *the teleological* disappear as the *we* appears. We have to work things out between each other before we get anything done. We come first.

...

space between us that is no longer walled off. It reaches others. That, ironically, becomes practical—the "first practical" of the person and so of community.

Circumvention stirs community through a kind of disappearance—the disappearance of the calculus of using people, the disappearance of invulnerability, perfection, and defense.

Presently absenting, then absently present, circumvention's movement is there within self-possession's comforting illusion, almost hidden unless you begin to be vulnerable with others.

And then, look, listen: there is disagreement rising, my friend. There is a wind in your chest, a shaking anxiety and a lost longing for something vaguely resembling personal intimacy and understanding ....

*

Dear friend,

Now is the time in this small book you hold in your hands (while possibly others observe you), where the book becomes lost! Everything has swiveled about like a weathervane in gale force weather, and this letter before your eyes is the book, the book the dream of the letter!

The beautiful speed of the wind has broken through the pages by shattering the order of narration. There is disagreement in our society of possessions.

There is disagreement in these pages.

I am speaking out of turn, delayed from this point on my porch, one summer evening in 2048, with the crickets cascading back and forth their call, their response, their call. And where are you?

Where are you, really?

Where are you? I am in a society of possessions. I am wrestling with community, and let me tell you, that means with politics, that major field of the practical as Aristotle thought. But both politics and community are in chaos in the society of possessions.

For instance, they are increasingly content with the word "militant." Many friends think that they must adopt militancy to be practical in this society of possessions with its vicious police state and its acts of increasing dispossession. My friends are ready to steel themselves as if they were *war-machines, robots of purpose,* to fight the society-of-possessions' current state.

It is a symptom of a wide disorder. I understand them, my friends, for some of us call each other this ("friends?"), not because we presume, but because we project. We are wish and assertion about the society in which we intend to live. Dashed hopes—brave folly. We do not want to live anymore in this society of possessions; we find that we have not been living well. The injustice cries out to us. It cries out on us and our fellows here on Earth. The injustice cries out. And what are we to *do*?

But we are misunderstanding politics, just as we misunderstand action and community. We are only political when we are people with *each* other—not threats, obstacles, playthings, toys, spectators, investments, resources, approvals, lackeys, tools, shoulders (always to cry on), fuckers, fucks, suckers, thieves, knives, tests, or trials. Nor enemies, even.

Such a realization is the first projection of community, a socialism of society before economy rules all. It goes: the society of possessions has kept us apart. Shall we circumvent?

And that is not something up to me. I have only a say in it, and so do you, only a say. The *relational* field of politics is not a strategy of forces. As a work of *community,* it sorts out what we will do and how we live here together. What world can we share?

From the standpoint of circumvention, the first, practical thing of politics is community, that is, it is *relationship*. The "politics" of forces is so much police, state or revolutionary, no matter.

Hear politics differently. You rarely find it in a newspaper, and it has no strategy. "Strategy" comes from the Greek *stratēgos*—to lead an army. It is military, just as the term "militant" is. It is *war teleology*. But, my friends, to be communal is not to wage war! Do not be confused by the society of possessions as it has seeped its way into the core of your hopes. Cast the teleologies of war to the void!

To circumvent self-ownership is to find the politics of relationships. The question is what it is to open the political from this point. "Politics of relationships" sounds cynical, more calculation, teleology, strategy. But hear "politics" differently.

You might think that a politics of relationships stays stuck in the policed realm of "private" life. Alongside it, it would be to believe in the "public" *merely* as the policed-in zone of containment where we get to act before each other.

But, no, there is a larger public, inside which the private is carried *with* us *as* our space of self-respect, not the place where abuse is permitted. In this public-private, our public is to seek *people*—to imagine *democracy*—as an openness between people in the moment when we must consider the norms that will be *our* will.

In *that* public, we carry the private within as the de*priva*tion of the calculations—the teleology of others mindless of our will. In that private, we carry the void inside us that is always a mystery in disappearance and in which there is always the unconditional privacy of respect. In *that* public, the private is always the underside of personal reality, as a dream is to night.

Hear "politics" differently as the multi-wise action: the private deprives the society of possessions of its claim to manipulate us in a field of objects, obstacles, and investments. The public brings people before each other as the space between *us* where *we* disagree to consider *us, our* will, even the norms we *will* share. The action is our meeting, negotiating, relating, disagreeing, and ... again!

Hear "politics" differently as the multi-wise: the norms we find through disagreement *cannot* be exclusive. If they are, they will not be open to disagreement, will try to possess it in advance. The whole "normative space" must rest in the fluidity of relationships or it will cease to circumvent.

Hear "politics" differently as the multi-wise relational: The political can never be reduced to a quality of the norms we share but must reside in the power of finding each other, across conflict and defended-ness, in an openness between each other. In and from this openness we can insist upon equality, as the void draws out all normality into a vacuum where community recreates the conditions of society from the delimiting edge of the unconditional. These moments are meetings and, as such, are dreams.

The dream of community against the exclusions of the society of possession is the figure of relationship. And even it cannot be imagined, friends, it cannot.

Your militancy, friends, is a mistake. It is invulnerability, strategy, calculus. **Politics is a vulnerability multi-wise held by all involved,** not a boardroom meeting, nor a clash at the barricades. A *personal* meeting: where we are now is not where we were once then. We had no idea that we *could* meet—yet alone in this way. The openness between us is vulnerability, thoughtfulness, and circumvention of the strategies. Will we work through conflict and the history of the erased crimes? Will we remain thoughtful and disagree?

I wish to hear you, too, or so I dream. Because of relating's surprise and politics' suctioning out of the normal, the politics of circumvention always begins as *protest*. It puts something to the test between people, stuttering the normal as a gust of wind causes limbs to instantly recoil, tossing about and losing their sense of settled place. Protest opens the cosmos between us to its grand contingency. This, we happen to call "society." But how should we live? Can I hear *you*? How do *I* deal with this challenge, this dispossession? How can we *hold* the disagreement?

Any mind is tossed about wildly by the challenge of multi-wise politics, by militancy, protest, and a community that is beyond the contingency of a society that keeps everyone in their place according to its calculus.

The militants of the society of possession say this: protest to *get* something, and no wonder, for oppression and negligence tear apart lives and livelihoods. But even the *things* are proxies for *relationship,* ontologically unkind to it, and so eventually no substitute. The *community* is the place beyond and before all things we might want, where our living together appears or is erased.

Circumvent this society and find the politics of community. Stop being "militants," o my friends. Be relatives.

~ Fritz Books, 76 years old, Shaker Heights, Ohio, September 4th, 2048

*

Something is moving, is unfixed, and I cannot hold onto this figure of my imagination, the "wind."

Nor is it abstract, this thing. I am moved by it, grapple with it, am lost. It slips through my mind as through my hands and fingers, running along the roots of my hair. It's a hole in my mind.

Like you.

*

It was not easy moving through my family's history after my mom's death. But I did. I moved fluidly. There was no way to contain it—trying to do so just ended in pain. I had to let the pain pass through me in my mourning and my patience with myself. I had done the hard part—I had broken with the society of possession.

The air was pouring into my house now, so to speak, and I shared my home with the wind.

Now, at the center of myself, was the sense that most things were empty outside of genuine relations—love, wonder, intimate talk, craft, honest questioning and curious knowing, self-abandonment to things open and beautiful that could not be boxed into strategies or hoarded. But these things that appeared in relations, they were also not substantial, because they were gifts. They were only there in the relating—as strange graces out of time, unexpected and in the acts.

These were the opposite of possessions: the friends I loved, the poems I crossed out and remade, the cities that appeared in fragments thanks to the poems and friends and love from out of the surrounding unease. Even my accounting homework was quiet and honest, the ledger having an evidence of its own that I could not control. I was not trying to screw people out of things. I was trying to be open and accountable.

Thus stillness was a freedom in the midst of pressure, as was light at the edges of otherwise impatient streets, the passing away then coming of life, uneasy in a still unjust world. So were classrooms with a strange, surprising clarity that jumped out at you from the midst of fatigue within the worknight tiredness, everyone's minds pressing close and the room suddenly awake. So were thoughts, and so, too, were demonstrations on Public Square downtown against completely unjustified police violence.

As I went to bed one night, I talked to myself in the dark. It was funny, but I was used to being a fool. I said, "You deserve to think about your life. It does not have to not make sense."

As I fell asleep, I remembered the lake in the mountains of Central New York one summer when my mother rented a cottage for myself and her cousins there. There were so many of us that summer, rich as a garden of many varieties of plants, cukes and all.

We played in the woods along the shore. The lake echoed voices from its glassy surface. A heron at the end circumvented all clamor and pegged its bony legs, one by one, into the muck, searching.

The light would stay until ten at night. Then the stars appeared in the lake's blackness out of the twilight purple.

I remembered the time I spent a summer in France thanks to the Rotary Club of Euclid, Ohio. That was the first and only summer I fell in love—something I could not find for such a long time—until I imploded and, much later, met you. I remembered walking toward the Place d'Opéra—the old opera house—with Anne-Christine in

Paris in late Fall 1988 or early March 1989. We were weathered companions - short-lived, a premonition of life after my undoing.

All these things were in the void, and, Antlers, I slept.

Shaker Heights, Ohio, September 2016

Thanks:
Misty Morrison
Cleveland, Ohio
David Keymer
Challenges to Recognition, Fall 2017
Emily Dragowski
Alex Shakar & Rana Khoury
Lynne Huffer
Sarah Gridley
Rachael Arrighi
Eileen Joy
Miton Leonn
Amir & Dzena Berbić
Lars Helge-Strand
Stephen M. Rich
Chloë Bass
Shaker Heights, Ohio
Kyle Powys Whyte
ECPR—Pisa, 2016
Steve Vogel
Amy Lynch
The Quarterly
Elaine Hullihen
Tony Tenaglier
Wilkinsburg, Pennsylvania
International Association of Environmental Philosophy
American Society for Aesthetics—Feminist Caucus

John Levy Barnard
Living Forms
Martha Nussbaum
Susan Neiman
The Yale Literary Magazine
Case Western Reserve University, Beamer-Schneider Professorship
Mike Andrews, *eFlux*
The Moral Inquiries
National Lawyer's Guild
Zirkus
Vincent W.J. van Gerven Oei
Renee Holland-Golphin
The *Oxford American Dictionary,* for many etymologies

www.ingramcontent.com/pod-product-compliance
Lightning Source LLC
Chambersburg PA
CBHW072046160426
43197CB00014B/2648